DIDO & ÆNEAS

HENRY PURCELL

Libretto by/*Libretto von*
Nahum Tate

Edited by/*Herausgegeben von*
Edward J. Dent

Revised Edition by/*Revidierte Ausgabe von*
Ellen T. Harris

German translation by/*Deutsche Übersetzung von*
A. Meyer

VOCAL SCORE / *KLAVIERAUSZUG*

The chorus score is also on sale
Die Chorpartitur ist ebenfalls käuflich erhältlich

Music Department
OXFORD UNIVERSITY PRESS
Oxford and New York

CONTENTS / *INHALT*

DRAMATIS PERSONAE

Dido	Soprano
Belinda	Soprano
Second Woman/*Zweite Frau*	Mezzo-soprano
Sorceress/*Zauberin*	Mezzo-soprano
First Witch/*Erste Hexe*	Soprano
Second Witch/*Zweite Hexe*	Soprano
Spirit/*Geist*	Soprano
Aeneas	Tenor or high baritone
First Sailor/*Erster Matrose*	Tenor
Chorus/*Chor*	

PREFACE

All Purcell lovers owe a large debt of gratitude to Edward J. Dent for his edition of *Dido and Aeneas* first published in 1925. His attempt to recreate Purcell's original score signalled the first such effort since the opera's appearance in 1689, and the continuing reliability of this edition testifies to Dent's scholarship and musicianship. In the light of new or newly available source information, however, the time has come to revise Dent's score. This task has been undertaken in the hope of reproducing the spirit of Dent's own efforts—that is, of providing a score that is both scholarly, representing the original as closely as possible, and practical for performers.

Dido and Aeneas was first performed in spring of 1689, as has been demonstrated by careful study of the opera's spoken epilogue which was published separately and refers to contemporary political events.[1] Purcell's own score does not survive and no seventeenth-century manuscript source of any kind exists, but a single printed libretto preserved in the library of the Royal College of Music, London, although undated, probably derives from the original performance. According to the libretto, this took place at a girls' school in Chelsea run by Josias Priest, a dancing master. In the libretto the opera begins with a mythological/pastoral prelude that allegorically honours the reigning English monarchs, William and Mary. There follow three equal acts beginning, respectively, with 'Shake the cloud', 'Wayward sisters', and 'Come away, fellow sailors'. The second act is divided into two equal scenes, the first for the witches in 'The Cave', the second, beginning with 'Thanks to these lonesome vales', in 'The Grove'. These act and scenic divisions become important because they are not duplicated in any of the later surviving sources.

After its performance at the Chelsea girls' school, *Dido* next appeared in an adaptation of Shakespeare's *Measure for Measure* (London, 1700); it was broken up and used, sometimes out of order, as entertainments at the ends of the acts. The first and third acts were not altered; in the second the two scenes were reversed and the Grove scene expanded. The Prologue was altered and expanded, and placed last.[2]

In 1704 *Dido* was again performed in London, apparently as a continuous whole and in the right order, as an epilogue to two separate plays.[3] No contemporary scores or librettos survive.

The first surviving score, the Tenbury manuscript (now housed in the Bodleian Library, Oxford), can be dated by its paper type to the second half of the eighteenth century. It is lacking the Prologue entirely, but the remainder of the opera is presented in the correct order, although the act divisions are different from those given in the libretto. The first act runs through the Cave scene, ending with the Echo Dance, where there is the designation 'End of Part I'. Act II then consists of only the Grove scene with no musical setting for the concluding chorus and dance given in the libretto. Act III is unchanged. This lopsided formal plan appears to represent a division of the opera into two equal parts (after the Echo Dance), a division which differs from the formal plans in either the 1689 libretto or the 1700 wordbook. Because the role of the second woman has been significantly reduced, and the elimination of one female part would make the cast list of *Dido* equal to that of John Eccles's masque *Mars and Venus*, which was performed with *Dido* in 1704, perhaps as a replacement for the prologue, it seems that the Tenbury manuscript probably derives from this performance. The score preserves a late seventeenth-century notational style, indicating that it was copied from a much earlier source now lost. As all succeeding manuscripts reproduce the formal plan of the Tenbury, they must all derive either from it or its source.

Librettos from 1774 (New York Public Library) and 1778 (Royal College of Music, Portrait Gallery) attest to concert performances of *Dido and Aeneas* given by the Academy of Ancient Music. Cuts and alterations in the text make it possible to identify the musical manuscripts connected with these performances: they include two scores in the British Library (Add. mss. 31450 and 15979), one at the Folger Shakespeare Library, Washington, DC (F770), and various sets of parts at the Royal Academy of Music, London (RAM 25). The musical adaptation to the facile rococo style makes these sources interesting documents in the history of stylistic change but of little use in preparing an edition of Purcell's music.

At about the same time as these performances, another copy of *Dido* was made which tends to reproduce the reading of the Tenbury score, but is modernized in the notation of time and key signatures, accidentals, and some stylistic details. An excellent secondary source, it is preserved by the National Trust at Tatton Park, Cheshire. The Tatton Park manuscript, copied by Philip Hayes, is dated 1784–5, and was probably copied from the same source used for the Tenbury.[4]

Finally there is the so-called Ohki Manuscript which once belonged to W. H. Cummings. It derives from the early part of the nineteenth century and is a collation of the Tenbury/Tatton readings and the Academy of Ancient Music scores; it is now preserved in the Nanki Music Library, Japan.[5] As the latest of the known manuscript scores, and one that derives in part from the altered concert version, it cannot be considered a reliable source.

After the Academy concerts in the 1770s and 1780s, no performances of *Dido* can be documented for almost a hundred years. However, in 1841 Alexander Macfarren published both a full and a vocal score of the concert version for the Musical Antiquarian Society, and this edition most probably spawned some performances even if documentation for them is now lacking. In 1888 William Cummings published a new edition that took into account the reading of his own score (Ohki) and the newly discovered Tenbury source, but as Edward J. Dent wrote in the preface to his 1925 edition, Cummings still overrated the value of the concert version. Nevertheless, this edition stimulated new interest in the score, and with the approach of the bicentenary of Purcell's death, performances began to accumulate; Liverpool (1877), Royal Academy of Music, London (1878), Bach Choir, London (1888), and finally a staged performance at the Royal College of Music, London (1895).

1 W. Barclay Squire, 'Purcell's *Dido and Aeneas*', *The Musical Times*, liv (1918), pp. 252–4; John Buttrey, 'Dating Purcell's *Dido and Aeneas*', *Proceedings of the Royal Musical Association*, xciv (1967–8), pp. 51–62; and Margaret Laurie (ed.), *Dido and Aeneas*, London 1979, p. ix.

2 Eric Walter White, 'New Light on *Dido and Aeneas*', in *Henry Purcell (1659–1695): Essays on his Music*, ed. Imogen Holst, London 1959, pp. 14–34.

3 *The London Stage (1660–1800)*, Part 2: 1700–1729, ed. Emmett L. Avery, Carbondale 1960, vol. I, p. 55 (*The Anatomist* by Edward Ravenscroft: 29 January 1704) and p. 63 (*The Man of Mode* by Sir George Etherege: 8 April 1704); also p. 58, where *Dido* is not mentioned by name but the description of '4 musical entertainments' and the mention of *Mars and Venus* implies the same musical additions as on 29 January (*The Anatomist*: 17 February 1704).

4 Nigel Fortune, 'A New Purcell Source', *Music Review*, xxv (1964), pp. 109–13.

5 Imogen Holst, 'A Note on the Nanki Collection of Purcell's Works', in *Henry Purcell (1659–1695)*, op. cit., Appendix C, pp. 127–30.

Dent's edition, based mainly on the Tenbury score, brought international recognition to Purcell's music. It included a German translation making it also accessible to German-speaking countries. The edition was used for a staged performance in Münster (1926), for the Austrian première (Vienna, 1927), Stuttgart (1927), Basle (1931), and so on. This edition was also used to introduce the staged version to the United States at the Juilliard School of Music, New York (1932), and for the Italian première (Florence, 1940), among others.

In recent years a great clamour has arisen about the apparently missing numbers at the end of the libretto's Act II. In the modern editions that have appeared since Dent's, edited by Imogen Holst and Benjamin Britten (1960) and by Margaret Laurie and Thurston Dart (1961), these have been supplied by fitting the existing words to other Purcell pieces or by writing new music for the chorus, and by adding an additional dance movement. This seems unnecessary for two reasons. First, no matter how carefully it is done, the addition of these pieces introduces a non-Purcellian element into a score that illustrates the composer at the top of his form; tampering with Purcell's delicate word-setting is especially problematic. But second, the additions are unnecessary even for the dramatic and tonal reasons adduced. If Aeneas and two of his sailors help Dido and the courtiers to exit during 'Haste, haste to town' [31], then their exit can be halted by the appearance of the spirit. The two sailors can stay until Aeneas's line 'Jove's commands shall be obey'd, Tonight our anchors shall be weigh'd', which can function as a command to them. Aeneas's soliloquy then provides the time span needed for the sailors to return to the ships and to begin telling their comrades the news ('Come away, fellow sailors'). The lack of music for the witches, therefore, does not affect the dramatic continuity of the plot; it also creates no problem tonally.

Dido is tonally constructed in six scenes each in its own key. Scene 1 ends with 'Whence could so much virtue spring' [6]; scene 2 begins with 'Fear no danger' [7] and runs to the 'Triumphing Dance' [15]. Scenes 3 and 4 correspond to the Cave scene and the Grove scene. Scene 5 begins with 'Come away, fellow sailors' [34] and runs to The Witches Dance [39]; scene 6 extends from 'See, Madam, see where the Prince appears' [40] to the end of the opera. The tonalities of these scenes are: C minor, C major, F minor-major, D minor-major, B-flat major, and G minor. In only a few cases are these keys interrupted.

During the Cave scene, for example, the sounds of the hunt (from the Grove scene) intrude upon the witches' plotting, and these interruptions occur in the D major-minor tonality of that scene (D major in the hunting horn calls of no. 20 and D minor in the witches' plan to disrupt the hunt with a storm, 'But ere we this perform' [22]). The only other interruptions relate directly to Aeneas. His entrance in scene 2 temporarily moves the tonality from C major to E minor (from the middle of no. 9 to the middle of no. 11), and his discussion with the spirit and the following monologue move the Grove scene from D major to A minor. Scenes 1, 5 and 6 are uninterrupted. By means of these tonal disturbances in otherwise stable scenes, Purcell indicates that Aeneas's actions cause disruption, just as the intrusion of the hunt upon the Cave scene is a disruption, and Aeneas's 'out-of-key' ending to the Grove scene is totally in keeping with his 'out-of-key' entrance in the second scene. The ending of the Grove scene (without the libretto's chorus and dance) also creates a perfectly symmetrical two-part form to the opera, as implied by the score, with Aeneas's monologue in scene 4 balancing Dido's 'Whence could so much virtue spring' at the end of scene 1. Whether this represents Purcell's intention, an alteration for the 1704 performances, or only a copying error cannot, however, be determined definitively. For those who insist on a tonal closure for scene 4, this edition suggests the simple repetition of the scene's opening D minor *Ritornelle*, a function even suggested by its name.

Performing material for this edition is available on hire from Oxford University Press. A companion miniature score is also published by Eulenburg.

EDITORIAL NOTES

Sources:

Libretto (LIB); Royal College of Music, London [1689].

Tenbury manuscript (TEN), full score [*c.*1775]; St Michael's College, Tenbury (now housed in the Bodleian Library, Oxford).

Tatton Park manuscript (TAT), full score [1784–5] copied by Philip Hayes; National Trust, Cheshire County Council.

The problem facing any editor of *Dido and Aeneas* is that there is no definitive source. The two best sources, the 1689 libretto and the Tenbury manuscript, suffer from serious shortcomings and discrepancies, and the editor must attempt to find the best reading by a careful collation of these. In musical matters the Tatton Park manuscript is also helpful, for it sometimes clarifies confused readings in the Tenbury. However, because it contains modernized time signatures (e.g. 3/4 for **3**), key signatures (e.g. three flats rather than two for C minor), accidentals (e.g. the ♮ replaces the ♭ and accidentals cover the measure rather than the note), and stylistic details (e.g. the elimination of the scotch snap rhythm by reversing the rhythmic values as on the phrase 'full of woe' in 'Whence could so much virtue spring' [6] and throughout 'Ah! Belinda' [3]), the Tatton Park readings remain secondary to those from Tenbury. The 1700 version, the manuscripts deriving from the Academy productions, and the Ohki manuscript are too altered to be useful. In this edition only the 1689 libretto, the Tenbury manuscript, and the Tatton Park manuscript have been collated. Textual notes may be found in the published orchestral scores.

The 1689 libretto and Tenbury manuscript

The formal discrepancies between these sources have been described above. In this edition the plan of the libretto has been given precedence, but the apparent two-part plan of the Tenbury manuscript is indicated editorially in brackets.

The authority of the musical source in the dispensation of musical forces has not been questioned in this edition, so that when, for example, the quatrain beginning 'But ere we this perform' [22] is assigned in the score to two witches as a duet, whereas in the libretto it is given to the Sorceress as an apparent solo, it has been assumed that this change originated with Purcell, and it is offered without commment.

This edition follows the role designations of the manuscript when there are obvious errors in the libretto, such as when the lines 'Aeneas has no fate but you. Let Dido smile, and I'le defie the feeble stroke of destiny', are given to Dido rather than Aeneas. In some cases, however, the role designations of the libretto seem preferable to those in the Tenbury manuscript. For example, in 'Whence could so much virtue spring' [6] Dido sings the opening quatrain in C minor. Belinda then enters with a closed couplet ('A tale so strong') in the minor dominant (G minor). The next couplet ('What stubborn heart'), which is set off by a distinct and abrupt change to the relative major (E-flat major), is assigned in the libretto to the Second Woman, whereas the musical sources indicate no change of part. The music, however, supports the libretto's reading and the eighteenth-century manuscripts may represent changes made for the 1704 performance, as discussed above.

Wherever possible the text of the opera has been taken from the libretto. Spellings and punctuation have been silently modernized where it was thought they might confuse, but the convention of identifying individual lines of verse with capitalization at the beginning and punctuation at the end has been retained. In general, immediate repetitions of lines or parts of lines are not capitalized; repetitions of whole lines preceded by an intervening line are.

The libretto offers stage directions throughout, which are here given complete. The sometimes more elaborate stage directions and titles from Tenbury, which may derive from the 1700 or 1704 performances, or both, are distinguished by being placed in parentheses. For example, the thunder and lightning called for in the Tenbury manuscript at the end of Act I does not appear in the libretto. It probably dates from the 1704 performance as the direction makes no sense unless the score is continuous at this point (as it is in the two-part division of the musical scores) leading directly into the scene with the witches.

At the end of the Cave scene, the libretto calls for a dance of the Inchantresses and Fairies; in the Tenbury score it has been changed to a dance for the Furies. This alteration is more than a mistake, as the direction at the end of the dance indicates, where there is a call for more thunder and lightning while the furies spectacularly rise and sink. Presumably these changes, too, derive from 1700 or 1704.

In some cases Tenbury offers more precise directions for the entrances of characters, for it was a seventeenth-century convention (which is generally followed throughout *Dido*) to list at the beginning of a scene all the characters that would enter during it and not to give specific entrances. Thus in the Grove scene, the characters are instructed to enter after the opening *Ritornelle*. In the last act, the sailors enter after the Prelude for 'Come away, fellow sailors', and in the same scene the Sorceress and Witches only enter at 'See, the flags and streamers curling'. These last directions imply either that the treble parts of 'Come away, fellow sailors' should be taken by the 'shore nymphs' who are being deserted (which seems dramatically unsound) or that the sailors sing all four parts. This is the only scene to call for two dramatically distinct four-part choruses—the sailors and the witches.

According to the libretto, Dido exits from the Grove scene after singing 'Haste, haste to town' [31]. Belinda and the chorus should exit by the end of the following chorus (which is lacking in the libretto). Although two or three of Aeneas's men may remain and hear 'Jove's command' (as happens in the 1700 version where they are given lines to sing), they should exit when Aeneas gives the command for the anchors to 'be weigh'd', leaving him alone on stage for the monologue.

The libretto also calls for a number of dances that seem to be lacking from the score. Most of these, however, were probably danced to a sung movement. For example, the Basque in Act I is certainly danced to 'Fear no danger' [8] as the libretto gives the indication: 'Dance this chorus'. Similarly, the 'Dance of the 2 drunken sailors' may occur during 'But ere we this perform' [22], and the *Cupids Dance* may occur during a repetition of the final chorus, 'With drooping wings' [44]. The Tenbury manuscript encloses this chorus in repeat marks without any indication of whether it is to be sung upon its repetition. In this edition an instrumental repetition as accompaniment to the *Cupids Dance* is assumed.

The pantomimed dance calling for a 'Jack of the Lanthorn' (or nightwatchman) to lead 'The Spaniards out of their way among the inchantresses' is surely represented by Tenbury's *Witches Dance* [39], which occurs at the same point. The pantomimed dance of the libretto belongs to the seventeenth-century tradition of antimasques (or comic *divertissements* before the entrance of the formal dancers), and occurs in the opera just before the scene leading to Dido's death. It would be appropriate that this dance be comic.

In Act I and during the Grove scene, guitar pieces over repetitive basses are indicated for dances. These were probably improvised in 1689. As they occur at important moments, however, it is dramatically useful to include something at these points. For the *Dance Gittars Chacony* [13] in Act I, this vocal score offers a harpsichord transcription (not a reduction) of the first six bass repetitions of the orchestral C major chaconne from Purcell's *Fairy Queen* (1692), based on the Royal Academy of Music manuscript and Ms. 1144 at the Royal College of Music, which includes bass and treble parts only. This dance may accompany Dido's pantomimed acceptance of Aeneas' suit, which action is otherwise lacking in the libretto. If this movement is not used, the music should be continuous, as in the Tenbury manuscript, between 'Pursue thy conquest' [12] and 'To the hills and the vales' [14]. Otherwise the tonic chord of no. 12 should coincide with the first chord of the dance, whose ending should coincide with the first measure of no. 14.

For *Gitter ground a Dance* [28], the harpsichord transcription of Purcell's 'Crown the altar', a D minor ground from *Celebrate this Festival* (1693, a Birthday ode for Queen Mary) in British Library, Egerton 2959 (f. 16), is offered with simplified ornamentation. It may be played during a pantomimed ceremony honouring the goddess Diana or simply to accompany a reorganization of characters on stage after the worship of Diana in 'Thanks to these lonesome vales' [27] and before the entertainment of 'Oft she visits' [29]. In the parts available for hire both dances are given in guitar transcriptions.

The Tenbury and Tatton Park manuscripts

Tenbury is the most important musical source and it has been closely followed in this edition. In the full score, however, the somewhat compacted Tenbury score has been expanded so that, for example, Belinda's staff at the end of 'Shake the cloud' [1] is extended through the first line of 'Banish sorrow' [2] and the necessary rest added without comment. The sharing of staves in Tenbury explains the occasions on which the instrumentation is clearly given: these indications only occur where a question might arise about the disposition of parts within the system. For example, at the beginning of 'Harm's our delight' [17] the first and second violins are specifically marked because they are written on a single staff. The orchestral indications for strings do not indicate that in other unmarked places wind instruments should be included. Rather they are a corroboration that the orchestral parts are for strings only.

Tenbury follows a late seventeenth-century style of notation. In the present edition key signatures have been modernized without comment (therefore corresponding to Tatton Park). Accidentals also have been changed to follow modern practice. Time signatures, however, have not been modernized and have been based on the Tenbury manuscript, for they have significance beyond the indication of metrical division: still closely tied to the old proportional system, they also indicate tempo. Thus the crotchet of c equals the minim of **2** equals the dotted minim of **3** and two dotted crotchets of 3/8. The proportions can be illustrated as follows: c ♩ = 2 𝅗𝅥 = 3 𝅗𝅥. = $\frac{3}{8}$ ♩. ♩.

1 : 2 : 3 : 6

Following this pattern the tempo of most pieces can be determined proportionally.

The system is most clearly seen in the short succession of movements beginning with 'Grief increases by concealing' [4]. If the tempo of this in c is taken at ♩=*c*. 66, then at the change to **2** for 'The greatest blessing' the tempo becomes 𝅗𝅥=66, and at 'When Monarchs unite' [5] the tempo is 𝅗𝅥.=66.

That is, one tactus governs all three metres and tempos. The three sections run on continuously in Tenbury with no breaks or double bars, and the upbeat in each case occurs in the tempo of the preceding section. In the present edition the look of unbroken continuity has been preserved throughout, and tempo relations are indicated editorially by showing which note value in the movement equals which note value of the preceding.

The proportional system of *Dido* is even clear in some of its failures. Tempo markings, for example, only occur where a change of tempo is desired within a single metre, as in the second half of the Overture or in Belinda's 'Pursue thy conquest, Love' [12], both of which are in *Quick* c rather than **2**. In the overture section a tempo equivalent to **2** works, and that tempo proportion has been suggested. This quick c tempo then holds through 'Banish sorrow' [2]. In 'Pursue thy conquest, Love', however, the tempo must fall between c and **2**; the *Quick* c in this case clearly specifies an alternate tempo to those provided by a time signature.

In 'Ah! Belinda' [3], Tenbury gives no metric sign even though the division changes from double in the preceding section to triple. The only marking is the tempo indication of *slow*. Apparently, the copyist was without a proper time signature for this tempo. The signature of **3** implied much too fast a tempo, yet, like **3**, the song contains three crotchets to the bar. The most logical choice would seem to be a slow 3/4, but this metre is used in Tenbury for *The Triumphing Dance* as an implied equivalent of **3**. As the copyist was left with no appropriate and available signature for the tempo of 'Ah! Belinda', he used the tempo marking instead. In the one other slow song in triple time, 'When I am laid in earth' [43], the signature 3/2 is used for the only time and relates to the proportional system in the ratio (3/2 𝅝.) = (c 𝅝); that is, bar equals bar.

The score contains other tempo-metric problems as well. In Act II, the Sorceress's recitation is given in **2** in 'Wayward sisters' [16] and 'The Queen of Carthage' [18]. In the third instance, however, in 'Ruin'd ere the set of sun'—'The Trojan Prince' [20], the time signature is c, but surely this section is not meant to be twice as slow as the preceding two. Assuming the tempo to be unchanged, it is then possible to take 'But ere we this perform' [22], which is marked as **2**, at what is effectively **1**, a much better tempo than **2** implies. Perhaps the copyist deliberately shifted levels. In this edition the time signatures from Tenbury have been preferred.

The one seemingly impossible time signature is the **3** of 'Our next motion' [37]. A slower tempo has been suggested. Throughout the edition, however, the continuity of the score has been emphasized. For example, Tenbury notates the measure that connects 'Destruction's our delight' [38] and *The Witches Dance* [39], both of which are in **2**, as follows: ♩ 𝅗𝅥 ‖ 𝄾 ♫♫

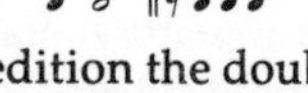

In this edition the double barline has been eliminated, as it so often is in Tenbury in similar junctures, as between 'But ere we this perform' [22] and 'In our deep vaulted cell' [23]. Similarly the shift in *The Witches Dance* from **3** back to ¢ (or 2) is notated: 3 ♩ 𝅗𝅥 ‖¢ ♪

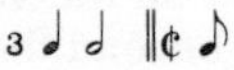

In this edition it appears as: ¢ ♩ 𝅗𝅥 [𝄾] ♪

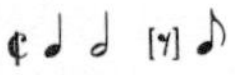

with the change of tempo (and metre) occurring in the last bar of the strain in **3**. In some other cases a single barline has been substituted for a thin double barline (after 2, 8, 10, 17, 19, 26, 31, 41), but no other notational alterations have been made.

The slurs, dynamic markings, and continuo figures (adjusted to modern key signatures) in this edition represent a conflation of the Tenbury and Tatton Park sources. In these matters both manuscripts are inconsistent, but they rarely contradict. For example, Tatton Park includes the indication *soft* over the continuo upbeat to 'But ere we this perform' [22]: Tenbury offers no dynamic marking, not a conflicting one. Thus the dynamic markings from both sources can be easily combined.

In the use of slurs, the purpose of this edition has not been either to regularize or follow a consistent pattern in all cases but to study the differences. Thus all vocal melismas are not automatically slurred. For example, the dotted melismas in 'Oft she visits' [29] are not slurred in either source. In 'Our next motion' [37], very similar dotted passages are slurred. If the tempos of the two pieces are taken into account then the appearance or lack of a slur would seem to point to distinctions in rhythmical performance. In the slow tempo of 'Oft she visits' (in c) with its walking bass, the dotted passages should be very pointed and probably overdotted. In the very fast 'Our next motion' (in **3**), however, the slurred dotted passages should most probably be performed closer to triplets than dotted figures. Thus in these cases the slurring distinction has been maintained as a clue towards rhythmic interpretation rather than legato or non-legato performance.

In a case similar to 'Our next motion', the chorus 'To the hills and the vales' [14] is also in **3** and contains many dotted melismas. In Tenbury only the last two notes of these passages are slurred: ♪. ♬. ♬. ♪| ♩

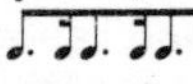

In Tatton Park the whole phrase is slurred. The present edition follows Tatton Park. The fast tempo at which this chorus should be performed will, as in 'Our next motion', turn the dotted figures into triplets. One should perhaps think of this movement as a wedding gigue. Not only the slurs, but the conflicting rhythmic notation of the upbeats (which is so typical of Baroque pieces written in double subdivision that demand a performance in triple subdivision) indicate a triplet rhythm. Thus in bar 9 the upbeat in all parts is in even quavers. In bar 20, however, at a repetition of the phrase, the upbeats are all dotted quavers and semiquavers, and at bar 35 the two versions are mixed throughout the parts and even on doubling parts (Violin II and Alto). These rhythmic inconsistencies have been maintained as an indication of the presumed performance of those passages in triplet rhythms. Such conflicts occur nowhere else in the score.

In an attempt to resolve the difficult problem of the continuo in a practical way, these companion editions present a variety of solutions. The vocal score contains a keyboard part that is partly reduction from the string parts, and partly realization, the latter given throughout in small notes. This score should thus be especially well-suited to reading, studying, and rehearsal. Although the hire full score contains no realization, the figures, which have been conflated from the Tenbury and Tatton Park sources, have been augmented by editorial figures in brackets. It is the hope of the editor that by providing a complete set of figures, improvised realizations will be encouraged. However, a short score with a full realization is also included with the parts in order not to hinder the performance of *Dido* by amateurs and school groups whose organizations this score has served so well. The published orchestral scores contain only those figures found in the Tenbury or Tatton Park sources.

The realizations are based on Dent's thus: those of the songs are essentially his, those of the choruses and dances (largely not provided by him) and the declamatory sections are essentially new. In all solo pieces melodic and dramatic considerations have been paramount. In the choruses and dances the realizations mainly provide a regular rhythmic pulse through simple harmonizations. Depending on the size of the hall, these can be augmented through the doubling of parts or the enlivening of the texture with quicker notes.

For more detailed discussions of the problems raised in the Preface and Editorial Notes, for musical analysis, a literary history and interpretation of the text, and a performance history, see the editor's forthcoming book on *Dido and Aeneas* (Oxford University Press).

The movements have been numbered editorially; in the vocal score editorial ties and slurs have a vertical stroke through them. Excepting these, all other editorial additions are shown in square brackets.

Ellen T. Harris

VORWORT

Alle Liebhaber der Musik Purcells sind Edward J. Dent für seine Ausgabe von *Dido und Aeneas*, die zuerst im Jahre 1925 erschien, zu großem Dank verpflichtet. Sein Versuch, die originale Partitur Purcells wiederherzustellen, war die erste derartige Bemühung seit dem Erscheinen der Oper im Jahre 1689, und die fortbestehende Zuverlässigkeit dieser Ausgabe ist ein Beweis für Dents Leistung als Gelehrter und Musiker. Nun ist jedoch, im Lichte neuen, oder seit kurzem verfügbaren Quellenmaterials, die Zeit gekommen, Dents Partitur zu revidieren. Diese Aufgabe wurde in der Hoffnung übernommen, den Geist der Bemühungen Dents wiederzuerzeugen, d.h. eine Partitur vorzulegen, die beides ist: musikwissenschaftlich fundiert, indem sie das Original so getreu wie möglich wiedergibt, und praktisch für die ausführenden Musiker.

Dido und Aeneas wurde im Frühjahr 1689 uraufgeführt, wie durch sorgfältige Untersuchungen des gesprochenen Epilogs der Oper nachgewiesen worden ist, der gesondert veröffentlicht wurde und auf politische Ereignisse der Zeit Bezug nimmt[1]. Purcells eigene Partitur ist nicht erhalten, und es existiert auch keinerlei handschriftliche Quelle aus dem 17. Jahrhundert. Aber ein einzelnes gedrucktes Libretto, das in der Bibliothek des Royal College of Music in London aufbewahrt wird, stammt, obgleich undatiert, vermutlich von der Erstaufführung her. Diese fand nach dem Libretto in einer Mädchenschule in Chelsea statt, die von Josias Priest, einem Tanzmeister, geleitet wurde. In dem Libretto beginnt die Oper mit einem mythologisch-pastoralen Vorspiel, das in allegorischer Form den regierenden Monarchen, William und Mary, huldigt. Es folgen drei gleichlange Akte beginnend mit „Laß die Stirne", „Düstre Schwestern" und „Kommt an Bord, ihr Matrosen". Der zweite Akt ist in zwei Szenen gleicher Länge unterteilt, die erste für die Hexen in der „Felsenhöhle" und die zweite, die mit „Dank Dir, Du Einsamkeit" anfängt, in der „Schlucht". Diese Akt- und Szeneneinteilungen gewinnen deshalb an Bedeutung, weil sie sich in keiner der aus späterer Zeit überlieferten Quellen wiederfinden.

Nach der Aufführung an der Mädchenschule in Chelsea wurde *Dido* das nächste Mal für Shakespeares *Measure for Measure* (London, 1700) adaptiert. Die Oper wurde zerstückelt und in mitunter veränderter Reihenfolge zu unterhaltsamen Einlagen am Ende der Akte benutzt. Der erste und der dritte Akt blieben unverändert, im zweiten Akt wurden die zwei Szenen vertauscht und die Schlucht-Szene erweitert. Der Prolog stand in veränderter und erweiterter Form am Schluß[2].

Offenbar als kontinuierliches Ganzes und in richtiger Reihenfolge wurde *Dido* 1704 in London als Epilog zu zwei verschiedenen Stücken wiederum aufgeführt[3]. Partituren oder Libretti aus dieser Zeit sind nicht erhalten.

Die erste überlieferte Partitur, die Tenbury-Handschrift (die jetzt in der Bodleian Library, Oxford, untergebracht ist), läßt sich anhand des Papiertyps auf die zweite Hälfte des 18. Jahrhunderts datieren. Hier fehlt der Prolog ganz, aber die übrige Oper wird in der richtigen Reihenfolge wiedergegeben, obwohl die Akteinteilungen von denen des Librettos abweichen. Der erste Akt reicht über die Höhlen-Szene hinaus und endet mit dem Echotanz, bei dem sich der Vermerk „Ende des I. Teils" findet. Der zweite Akt besteht daher lediglich aus der Schlucht-Szene ohne die Musik für den im Libretto vorgegebenen abschließenden Chor und Tanz. Akt III bleibt unverändert. Dieser unausgewogene Formplan scheint eine Teilung der Oper (nach dem Echotanz) in zwei gleiche Teile darzustellen, eine Unterteilung, die sowohl von dem Libretto von 1689 als auch von dem Workbook von 1700 abweicht. Da die Rolle der Zweiten Frau bedeutend gekürzt ist und die Auslassung einer weiteren weiblichen Partie die Besetzung von *Dido* derjenigen von John Eccles' Komposition *Mars and Venus* angleicht, die 1704 zusammen mit *Dido* aufgeführt wurde, vielleicht als Ersatz für den Prolog, hat es den Anschein, daß die Tenbury-Handschrift möglicherweise von dieser Aufführung herrührt. Die Partitur behält die Notationsweise des späten 17. Jahrhunderts bei, was darauf hindeutet, daß sie von einer viel früheren, heute verlorenen Quelle abgeschrieben wurde. Da alle nachfolgenden Handschriften den Formplan der Tenbury-Handschrift wiedergeben, müssen sie alle von ihr oder ihrer Quelle abstammen.

Libretti von 1774 (New York Public Library) und 1787 (Royal College of Music, Portrait Gallery) zeugen von konzertanten Aufführungen von *Dido und Aeneas* durch die Academy of Ancient Music. Streichungen und Änderungen im Text ermöglichen die Identifikation der Musikhandschriften, die mit diesen Aufführungen in Zusammenhang stehen. Zu ihnen gehören zwei Partituren in der British Library (Add. mss. 31450 und 15979), eine in der Folger Shakespeare Library, Washington, DC. (F 770), und verschiedene Stimmsätze in der Royal Academy of Music, London (RAM 25). Die musikalische Angleichung an den leichten Rokokostil macht diese Quellen zu interessanten Dokumenten für die Geschichte des Stilwandels, bringt aber wenig Nutzen bei der Vorbereitung einer Purcell-Ausgabe.

Etwa zur Zeit dieser Aufführungen wurde eine weitere Abschrift von *Dido* angefertigt, die in der Tendenz der Lesart der Tenbury-Handschrift folgt, jedoch in der Notationsweise des Taktes, der Schlüssel, der Vorzeichen und einiger stilistischer Details modernisiert ist. Diese ausgezeichnete Sekundärquelle wird vom National Trust in Tatton Park, Cheshire, aufbewahrt. Die von Philip Hayes kopierte Tatton Park-Handschrift ist auf 1784/85 datiert und wurde vermutlich von derselben Quelle abgeschrieben, die für die Tenbury-Handschrift benutzt wurde[4].

Schließlich gibt es noch die sogenannte Ohki-Handschrift, die ehemals W. H. Cummings gehörte. Sie stammt aus dem

---

1 W. Barclay Squire, „Purcell's *Dido and Aeneas*", *The Musical Times*, LIV (1918). S. 252–4; John Buttrey, „Dating Purcell's *Dido and Aeneas*", *Proceedings of the Royal Musical Association*, XCIV (1967–8), S. 51–62; und Margaret Laurie (Hg.), *Dido and Aeneas*, London 1979, S. ix.

2 Eric Walter White, „New Light on *Dido and Aeneas*", in: *Henry Purcell (1659–1695): Essays on his Music*, hg. von Imogen Holst, London 1959, S. 14–34.

3 *The London Stage (1660–1800)*, Teil 2: 1700–1729, hg. von Emmett L. Avery, Carbondale 1960, Bd. I, S. 55 (*The Anatomist* von Edward Ravenscroft: 29. Januar 1704) und S. 63 (*The Man of Mode* von Sir George Etherege: 8. April 1704); auch S. 58, wo *Dido* namentlich nicht erwähnt wird, aber die Beschreibung der „4 musical entertainments" [4 musikalischen Zwischenspiele, d. Übers.] und die Erwähnung von *Mars and Venus* impliziert, daß es sich um dieselben Musikbeigaben wie am 29. Januar handelt (*The Anatomist:* 17. Februar 1704).

4 Nigel Fortune, „A New Purcell Source", *Music Review*, XXV (1964), S. 109–13.

frühen 19. Jahrhundert, und in ihr sind die Lesarten der Handschriften von Tenbury und Tatton Park sowie der Partituren der Academy of Ancient Music kollationiert. Sie wird jetzt in der Nanki Music Library in Japan aufbewahrt[5]. Als jüngste der bekannten handschriftlichen Partituren, die auch zum Teil noch auf der veränderten Konzertfassung fußt, ist sie nicht als verläßliche Quelle anzusehen.

Nach den Akademie-Konzerten in den siebziger und achtziger Jahren des 18. Jahrhunderts lassen sich fast hundert Jahre lang keine weiteren Aufführungen belegen. Doch publizierte Alexander Macfarren 1841 für die Musical Antiquarian Society von der Konzertfassung sowohl eine Dirigier- als auch eine Vokalpartitur, und wahrscheinlich führte diese Ausgabe zu einigen Aufführungen, selbst wenn heute Belege dafür fehlen. 1888 veröffentlichte William Cummings eine neue Ausgabe, die der Lesart seiner eigenen Partitur (Ohki) und der neu entdeckten Tenbury-Quelle Rechnung trug, aber noch immer die Konzertfassung überbewertete, wie Edward J. Dent im Vorwort zu seiner Ausgabe von 1925 schrieb. Dessen ungeachtet rief diese Ausgabe ein neues Interesse an der Partitur hervor, und da sich Purcells zweihundertster Todestag näherte, begannen sich die Aufführungen zu häufen: Liverpool (1877), Royal Academy of Music, London (1878), Bach Choir, London (1888) und schließlich eine szenische Aufführung im Royal College of Music, London (1895).

Dents Ausgabe, die sich hauptsächlich auf die Tenbury-Handschrift stützt, brachte Purcells Musik internationale Anerkennung. Sie enthält eine deutsche Übersetzung, die sie auch den deutschsprachigen Ländern zugänglich machte. Die Ausgabe wurde für eine Bühnenaufführung in Münster (1926), für die österreichische Erstaufführung (Wien, 1927), für Aufführungen in Stuttgart (1927), Basel (1931) usw. benutzt. Sie diente auch zur Einführung der Bühnenfassung in den USA an der Juilliard School of Music, New York (1932) und unter anderem für die italienische Erstaufführung (Florenz, 1940).

In den letzten Jahren ist viel Lärm um die beiden Nummern am Ende des zweiten Aktes des Librettos entstanden, die offensichtlich fehlen. In den modernen, seit Dents Edition erschienen Ausgaben, die von Imogen Holst und Benjamin Britten (1960) und von Margaret Laurie und Thurston Dart (1961) herausgegeben wurden, sind sie bereitgestellt worden, indem die existierenden Worte anderen Stücken von Purcell unterlegt wurden oder neue Musik für den Chor hinzukomponiert und ein zusätzlicher Tanz beigefügt wurde. Dies scheint aus zweierlei Gründen unnötig. Zum ersten führt die Beifügung dieser Stücke, so sorgfältig sie auch geschehen sein mag, ein fremdes, nicht von Purcell stammendes Element in eine Partitur ein, die den Komponisten auf der Höhe seines Könnens zeigt—die Einmischung in Purcells feinfühlige Textbehandlung ist besonders problematisch. Aber zum zweiten sind die Beifügungen selbst aus den angeführten dramatischen und musikalischen Gründen nicht nötig. Wenn Aeneas und zwei seiner Matrosen Dido und ihren Höflingen während des „Schnell, schnell zur Stadt" [31] beim Abgang behilflich sind, so kann ihr eigener durch das Erscheinen des Geistes aufgehalten werden. Die zwei Matrosen können bis zu Aeneas' Zeile „Zeus'-Befehlen gilt mein Leben, Heut' Nacht laßt uns die Anker heben" bleiben, die als Befehl an sie fungieren kann. Aeneas' Selbstgespräch schafft sodann die Zeitspanne, die die Matrosen benötigen, um zum Schiff zurückzukehren und damit anzufangen, ihren Kameraden die Neuigkeit zu erzählen („Kommt an Bord, ihr Matrosen"). Wenn also die Musik für die Hexen fehlt, hat das keine Auswirkung auf den dramatischen Fortgang der Handlung; ein musikalisches Problem entsteht ebenfalls nicht.

Dido ist von den Tonarten her in sechs Szenen aufgebaut. Szene 1 endet mit „Von tapfren Ahnen er entsprang" [6]; Szene 2 beginnt mit „Fürcht' nicht, daß Gefahr erschien" [7] und geht bis zum „Siegestanz" [15]. Die Szenen 3 und 4 entsprechen der „Felsenhöhle" und der „Schlucht". Szene 5 fängt an mit „Kommt an Bord, ihr Matrosen" [34] und geht bis zum „Tanz der Hexen" [39]; Szene 6 erstreckt sich von „Sieh, Dido, dort Aeneas kommt" [40] bis zum Schluß der Oper. Die Tonarten der Szenen sind: c-Moll, C-Dur, f-Moll/F-Dur, d-Moll/D-Dur, B-Dur und g-Moll. Diese Tonarten werden nur in wenigen Fällen durchbrochen.

Während der Felsenhöhlen-Szene mischen sich zum Beispiel Jagdklänge (aus der Schlucht-Szene) in die Intrige der Hexen, und diese Unterbrechungen ereignen sich in dem d-Moll/D-Dur-Bereich jener Szene (D-Dur in den Jagdhornrufen von Nr. 20 und d-Moll in dem Plan der Hexen, die Jagd durch einen Gewittersturm zu stören, „Doch eh' wir dieses tun" [22]). Die einzigen anderen Unterbrechungen stehen in direkter Beziehung zu Aeneas. Bei seinem Auftritt in der zweiten Szene wechselt die Tonart zeitweilig von C-Dur nach e-Moll (von der Mitte von Nr. 9 bis zur Mitte von Nr. 11), und seine Unterhaltung mit dem Geist und der anschließende Monolog lassen die Schlucht-Szene von D-Dur nach a-Moll wechseln. Die Szenen 1, 5 und 6 werden nicht unterbrochen. Mittels dieser Störungen der Tonarten in sonst festgefügten Szenen deutet Purcell an, daß Aeneas' Handlungsweise Störung verursacht, ebenso wie das Eindringen der Jagd in die Schlucht-Szene. Und daß Aeneas die Schlucht-Szene in einer „falschen" Stimmung [d.h. in einer von der regulären abweichenden Tonart, d. Übers.] beschließt, paßt völlig zu seinem „falsch gestimmten" Auftritt in der zweiten Szene. Der Schluß der Schlucht-Szene (ohne den im Libretto vorgesehenen Chor und Tanz) verschafft der Oper auch eine vollkommen symmetrische, zweiteilige Form, wie in der Tenbury-Partitur impliziert, wobei Aeneas' Monolog in Szene 4 seine Entsprechung in Didos „Von tapfren Ahnen er entsprang" am Ende der Szene 1 findet. Ob dies Purcells Intentionen entspricht oder nur eine Änderung für die Aufführungen von 1704 darstellt oder lediglich einen Fehler in der Abschrift, läßt sich allerdings nicht endgültig entscheiden. Denjenigen, die auf einem Schluß in der richtigen Tonart bestehen, schlägt diese Ausgabe vor, das *Ritornell* in d-Moll vom Anfang der Szene zu wiederholen, eine Funktion, die der Name sogar nahelegt.

Aufführungsmaterial für diese Ausgabe ist leihweise von Oxford University Press erhältlich. Eine begleitende Taschenpartitur ist auch bei Eulenburg erschienen.

REVISIONSBERICHT

Quellen:

Libretto (LIB), Royal College of Music, London [1689].

Tenbury-Handschrift (TEN), vollständige Partitur [ca. 1775]; St. Michael's College, Tenbury (jetzt aufbewahrt in der Bodleian Library, Oxford).

Tatton Park-Handschrift (TAT), vollständige Partitur [1784–5], kopiert von Philip Hayes; National Trust, Cheshire County Council.

Jeder Herausgeber von *Dido und Aeneas* sieht sich vor das Problem gestellt, daß es keine definitive Quelle gibt. Die

[5] Imogen Holst, „A Note on the Nanki Collection of Purcell's Works", in: *Henry Purcell (1659–1695)*, a.a. O., Appendix C, S. 127–30.

beiden besten Quellen, das Libretto von 1689 und die Tenbury-Handschrift, leiden unter ernsten Mängeln und Widersprüchlichkeiten, und der Herausgeber muß die beste Lesart durch sorgfältiges Vergleichen herausfinden. In musikalischer Hinsicht ist auch die Tatton Park-Handschrift hilfreich, denn sie klärt mitunter Stellen, deren Lesart in der Tenbury-Handschrift unklar ist. Da sie jedoch modernisierte Taktvorzeichnungen (z.B. 3/4 statt **3**), Tonartenvorzeichnungen (z.B. eher drei statt zwei ♭ für c-Moll), Akzidentien (z.B. ♭ wird durch ♮ ersetzt, Vorzeichen gelten eher für den ganzen Takt als für die einzelne Note) und stilistische Details (z.B. die Eliminierung des Rhythmus' der sogenannten scotch snap [die Folge von kurzer, auf betontem Taktteil stehender Note mit nachfolgender längerer—vergleichbar dem lombardischen Rhythmus; d. Übers.] durch Verkehrung der rhythmischen Werte wie auf den Worten „voller Schmerz" in „Von tapfren Ahnen er entsprang" [6] und durchweg in „Ah! Belinda" [3]) enthält, bleiben die Lesarten von Tatton Park der Tenbury-Handschrift untergeordnet. Die Fassung von 1700, die Handschriften, die von den Academy-Aufführungen stammen, und die Ohki-Handschrift sind zu stark verändert, um nützlich zu sein. In dieser Ausgabe sind nur das Libretto von 1689, die Tenbury-Handschrift und die Tatton Park-Handschrift verglichen worden. Anmerkungen zum Text sind in den veröffentlichten Orchesterpartituren zu finden.

Das Libretto von 1689 und die Tenbury-Handschrift

Die formalen Abweichungen zwischen diesen Quellen sind weiter oben schon beschrieben worden. In dieser Ausgabe hat der Formplan des Librettos Vorrang erhalten, aber auf die offensichtlich zweiteilige Anlage der Tenbury-Handschrift wird vom Herausgeber in Klammern hingewiesen.

Hinsichtlich der musikalischen Kräfteverteilung ist die Autorität der Musikquelle in dieser Ausgabe nicht angezweifelt worden. Wenn zum Beispiel der Vierzeiler mit dem Anfang „Doch eh' wir dieses tun" [22] in der Partitur den zwei Hexen für ein Duett zugewiesen wird, wogegen ihn im Libretto die Zauberin offensichtlich als Solo erhält, so ist anzunehmen, daß diese Änderung auf Purcell zurückgeht, und daher wird sie nicht kommentiert.

Im Falle offensichtlicher Fehler im Libretto folgt diese Ausgabe den Rollenverteilungen der Handschrift, etwa wenn die Zeilen „Aeneas kennt kein Los als Dich. Wenn Dido lacht, bin ich gefeit Vor schwachen Schicksals Schlag und Leid" lieber Dido als Aeneas zugeteilt werden. Allerdings sind in manchen Fällen die Rollenzuweisungen des Librettos denen der Tenbury-Handschrift vorzuziehen. So singt zum Beispiel Dido in „Von tapfren Ahnen er entsprang" [6] die ersten vier Zeilen in c-Moll. Darauf tritt Belinda ein mit einem geschlossenen Zweizeiler („Ein starkes Lied") in der Moll-Dominante (g-Moll). Das nächste Reimpaar („Kein hart Gemüt"), das durch einen plötzlichen und deutlichen Wechsel in die verwandte Durtonart (Es-Dur) abgesetzt ist, wird im Libretto der Zweiten Frau zugewiesen, wogegen die Partitur keinen Wechsel der Partie anzeigt. Die Musik unterstützt jedoch die Lesart des Librettos, und die Handschriften aus dem 18. Jahrhundert sind vielleicht veränderte Fassungen für die Aufführungen von 1704, wie oben erläutert.

Wo immer möglich, wurde der Operntext aus dem Libretto gewählt. Rechtschreibung und Zeichensetzung sind dort stillschweigend modernisiert worden, wo sie zu Unklarheiten Anlaß gegeben hätten. Aber der Brauch, die einzelnen Verszeilen durch Großschreibung am Anfang und Satzzeichen am Ende kenntlich zu machen, wurde beibehalten. Im allgemeinen sind unmittelbar wiederholte Zeilen oder Zeilenbruchstücke am Anfang nicht großgeschrieben, hingegen ganze Wiederholungszeilen, denen Einschübe vorausgehen, doch.

Durch das ganze Libretto ziehen sich Bühnenanweisungen, die hier vollständig wiedergegeben sind. Die mitunter ausführlicheren Bühnenanweisungen und Überschriften der Tenbury-Handschrift, die vielleicht von den Aufführungen in den Jahren 1700 oder 1704 oder von beiden stammen, werden durch Parenthesen abgesetzt. So erscheinen zum Beispiel Donner und Blitz, die in der Tenbury-Handschrift am Ende des ersten Aktes verlangt werden, nicht im Libretto. Die Anweisung stammt vermutlich aus der Aufführung von 1704, denn sie ist nur sinnvoll, wenn an dieser Stelle die Partitur weiterläuft (wie es bei der Zweiteilung der Partituren geschieht) und direkt in die Hexenszene übergeht.

Am Ende der Höhlen-Szene verlangt das Libretto einen Tanz der Zauberinnen und Feen; in der Tenbury-Partitur ist daraus ein Furientanz geworden. In dieser Änderung steckt mehr als bloß ein Fehler, wie die Anweisung am Ende des Tanzes zeigt, denn dort wird mehr Blitz und Donner gefordert, während die Furien effektvoll auf- und niedersteigen. Vermutlich stammen auch diese Änderungen von 1700 oder 1704.

In einigen Fällen gibt die Tenbury-Handschrift genauere Anweisungen für die Personenauftritte, denn es war im 17. Jahrhundert üblich (*Dido* hält sich offensichtlich durchweg daran), zu Beginn einer Szene alle Personen aufzuführen, die in ihr erscheinen sollten, und nicht die einzelnen Auftritte anzugeben. So werden in der Schlucht-Szene die Personen angewiesen, nach dem Eingangs-Ritornell aufzutreten. Im letzten Akt kommen die Matrosen nach dem Vorspiel zu „Kommt an Bord, ihr Matrosen" herein, und in derselben Szene treten die Zauberin und die Hexen erst bei „Sieh die Flaggen, Wimpel wehen" auf. Die letzten Anweisungen implizieren, daß die Diskantpartien von „Kommt an Bord, ihr Matrosen" entweder die Landnymphen, die soeben verlassen werden, übernehmen (was dramatisch unsinnig erscheint) oder daß die Matrosen alle vier Stimmen singen. Dies ist die einzige Szene, die aus dramatischen Gründen zwei getrennte vierstimmige Chöre erfordert, einen Chor der Matrosen und einen Chor der Hexen.

Dem Libretto zufolge tritt Dido von der Schlucht-Szene ab, nachdem sie „Schnell, schnell zur Stadt" [31] gesungen hat. Belinda und der Chor sollten nach dem darauffolgenden Chor, der im Libretto fehlt, die Bühne verlassen. Obwohl zwei oder drei von Aeneas' Leuten zurückbleiben und „Zeus' Befehl" mitanhören können (wie es in der Fassung von 1700 tatsächlich geschieht, wo sie nämlich Zeilen zu singen haben), sollten sie doch abtreten, wenn Aeneas den Befehl gibt, die Anker „zu heben", und ihn für den Monolog auf der Bühne allein lassen.

Das Libretto verlangt auch eine Anzahl von Tänzen, die in der Partitur zu fehlen scheinen. Indessen wurden die meisten davon vermutlich zu einem gesungenen Satz getanzt. Die Basque im ersten Akt, zum Beispiel, wird sicherlich auf „Fürcht' nicht, daß Gefahr erschien" [8] getanzt, weil das Libretto den Hinweis „Diesen Chor tanzen" gibt. Auf ähnliche Weise mag der „Tanz der 2 betrunkenen Matrosen" während „Doch eh' wir dieses tun" [22] stattfinden, und der *Amorettentanz* während der Wiederholung des Schlußchors „In sanftem Flug" [44]. In der Tenbury-Handschrift ist dieser Chor zwischen Wiederholungszeichen gesetzt ohne einen Hinweis darauf, ob er bei der Wiederholung gesungen werden soll. In dieser Ausgabe wird von einer rein instrumentalen Wiederholung als Begleitung zum *Amorettentanz* ausgegangen.

Die Tanzpantomime, in der nach einem „Jack of the Lanthorn" (oder Nachtwächter) verlangt wird, der „die Spanier vom Wege ab unter die Zauberinnen" führen soll, ist mit Sicherheit im *Hexentanz* [39] der Tenbury-Handschrift präsent, der sich an derselben Stelle befindet. Die Tanzpantomime des Librettos steht in der Tradition der Anti-Masque (oder des heiteren Zwischenspiels vor dem Auftritt der ernsten, förmlichen Tänzer) des 17. Jahrhunderts und kommt in dieser Oper unmittelbar vor der Szene, die zu

Didos Tod führt. Komik wäre diesem Tanz angemessen.

In Akt I und in der Schlucht-Szene sind Gitarren-Stücke über wiederkehrenden Baßfiguren für Tänze angezeigt. Diese wurden 1689 vermutlich improvisiert. Da sie jedoch an wichtigen Stellen vorkommen, ist es, vom dramatischen Gesichtspunkt her gesehen, zweckdienlich, hier etwas einzufügen. Für den *Gitarrentanz* [13] in Akt I bietet dieser Klavierauszug eine Cembalo-Transkription (keinen Auszug) der ersten sechs Wiederholungen des Baßthemas der orchestralen Chaconne in C-Dur aus Purcells *Fairy Queen* (1692), der die Handschrift der Royal Academy of Music und Ms. 1144 des Royal College of Music, die nur Baß- und Sopranstimme besitzt, zugrunde liegen. Dieser Tanz kann Didos pantomimisch dargestellte Annahme von Aeneas' Werbung begleiten, eine Handlung, die sonst nicht im Libretto vorkommt. Wird dieser Satz nicht verwendet, so sollte die Musik, wie in der Tenbury-Handschrift, zwischen 'Die Liebe hat gesiegt' [12] und 'Euch Hügeln und Buchten' [14] fortlaufend sein. Andernfalls sollte der Tonika-Akkord von Nr. 12 mit dem ersten Akkord des Tanzes zusammenfallen, dessen Schluß wiederum sich mit dem ersten Takt von Nr. 14 decken sollte.

Für den *Gitarrentanz* [28] wird die Cembalo-Transkription von Purcells 'Kröne den Altar', einem Ground in d-moll aus *Celebrate this Festival* (einer Geburtstagsode für Königin Mary 1693) mit vereinfachter Ornamentierung angeboten (in der British Library, Egerton 2959 f. 16). Das Stück kann während einer pantomimisch dargestellten Zeremonie zu Ehren der Göttin Diana gespielt werden, oder einfach um eine Neuanordung der Personen auf der Bühne nach der Anbetung der Diana mit 'Dank Dir, Du Einsamkeit' [27] und vor dem Tanz von 'Oft an lieber Berge Stelle' [29] zu begleiten. Die leihweise erhältlichen Stimmen bieten beide Tänze in Transkriptionen für Gitarre.

Die Handschriften von Tenbury und Tatton Park

Die Tenbury-Handschrift ist die wichtigste Quelle für den Notentext, und ihr ist diese Ausgabe dicht gefolgt. Allerdings wurde die etwas zusammengedrängte Tenbury-Partitur um der Klarheit willen erweitert, so daß zum Beispiel Belindas Liniensystem am Ende von „Laß die Stirne" [1] noch über der ersten Zeile von „Fort mit Sorgen" [2] weitergeht und der notwendige Rest ohne Kommentar zugefügt wird. Aus der Teilung der Systeme in der Tenbury-Handschrift erklärt sich auch, daß bei anderen Gelegenheiten die Instrumentation ausdrücklich angegeben wird. Diese Hinweise erfolgen aber nur, wo Fragen zur Stimmdisposition innerhalb eines Systems entstehen könnten. So sind etwa am Anfang von „Tod unser Glück" [17] die ersten und zweiten Violinen besonders gekennzeichnet, weil sie auf nur einem Liniensystem notiert sind. Die Angabe von Streichern in den rein instrumentalen Teilen weist nicht darauf hin, daß an anderen Stellen ohne besonderen Vermerk Bläser mit einbegriffen sein sollten. Sie bestätigt vielmehr, daß die rein instrumentalen Partien nur für Streicher sind.

Die Tenbury-Handschrift folgt der Notationsweise des ausgehenden 17. Jahrhunderts. In der vorliegenden Ausgabe sind die Schlüsselvorzeichnungen kommentarlos modernisiert worden (und entsprechen somit der Tatton Park-Handschrift). Vorzeichen sind ebenfalls der modernen Praxis folgend geändert worden. Dagegen blieben die Taktvorzeichnungen unverändert und basieren auf der Tenbury-Handschrift, denn sie haben über die metrische Einteilung hinaus Bedeutung: noch eng dem alten Proportionssystem verhaftet, zeigen sie auch das Tempo an. So entspricht das Viertel in c der Halben in **2**, der punktierten Halben in **3** und zwei punktierten Vierteln im 3/8-Takt. Die Proportionen lassen sich folgendermaßen darstellen: c ♩ = 2 𝅗𝅥 = 3 𝅗𝅥. = 3/8 ♩. ♩.
1 : 2 : 3 : 6

Nach diesem Muster kann man das Tempo der meisten Stücke proportional bestimmen.

Das System wird am deutlichsten in der kurzen Folge von Abschnitten, die mit „Leid wird größer in der Stille" [4] beginnt. Wird das Tempo dieses ersten Abschnitts im c mit ♩=*ca.* 66 genommen, dann wird es bei „Zum größten Glück" im **2**er-Takt zu 𝅗𝅥=66, und bei „Wenn Herrscher vereint" [5] ist das Tempo 𝅗𝅥.=66. Das heißt, ein Grundschlag beherrscht alle drei Taktarten und Tempi. Die drei Abschnitte gehen in der Tenbury-Handschrift ohne Unterbrechung oder Doppelstriche ineinander über, wobei der Auftakt jedes Mal im Tempo des vorangegangenen Abschnitts genommen wird. In der vorliegenden Ausgabe ist die ungebrochene Kontinuität optisch durchweg beibehalten worden, und die Temporelationen sind vom Herausgeber vermerkt worden, indem er zeigt, welcher Notenwert im neuen welchem Notenwert im vorausgegangenen Satz entspricht.

Das Proportionssystem wird selbst dann deutlich, wenn es hin und wieder nicht aufgeht. Tempoangaben kommen zum Beispiel nur dort vor, wo ein Tempowechsel innerhalb derselben Taktart gewünscht wird wie in der zweiten Hälfte der Ouvertüre oder in Belindas „Die Liebe hat gesiegt" [12]. Beide Abschnitte stehen eher im *schnellen* c als im **2**. Im Ouvertüren-Abschnitt geht ein dem **2**er-Takt entsprechendes Tempo gut, und diese Tempoproportion wurde vorgeschlagen. Dieses schnelle c Tempo hält dann durch „Fort mit Sorgen" [2] hindurch an. In „Die Liebe hat gesiegt" hingegen muß das Tempo zwischen c und **2** liegen. Der *schnelle* c verlangt in diesem Fall deutlich ein anderes als durch die Taktvorzeichnung gegebenes Tempo.

In „Ah! Belinda" [3] hat die Tenbury-Handschrift keine Taktangabe, obwohl gegenüber dem vorausgegangenen Abschnitt die metrische Unterteilung von zwei zu drei wechselt. Den einzigen Vermerk bildet die Tempoangabe *langsam*. Offensichtlich hatte der Kopist keine geeignete Vorzeichnung für dieses Tempo zur Verfügung. Die Vorzeichnung einer **3** implizierte ein viel zu schnelles Tempo, und doch enthält dieses Lied, ähnlich dem **3**, drei Viertel pro Takt. Am logischsten würde die Wahl eines langsamen 3/4-Takts erscheinen, aber dieser Takt wird in der Tenbury-Handschrift für den *Siegestanz* als dem **3** implizit gleichwertig verwendet. Da dem Kopisten keine angemessene und verfügbare Taktvorzeichnung für das Tempo von „Ah! Belinda" blieb, benutzte er statt dessen die Tempobezeichnung. In dem einzigen weiteren langsamen Lied im **3**er-Metrum, „Werd' ich ins Grab gelegt" [43], kommt die Vorzeichnung 3/2 das einzige Mal zur Anwendung und bezieht sich auf das Proportionssystem im Verhältnis (3/2 𝅝.) = (c 𝅝), d.h. Takt gleich Takt.

Die Partitur birgt auch noch andere Probleme. Dem rezitativischen Gesang der Zauberin im zweiten Akt ist in „Düstre Schwestern" [16] und „Karthagos Herrin" [18] je eine **2** vorgezeichnet. Im dritten Fall jedoch, in „Heut' schon eh' die Sonne sinkt" — „Aeneas wurde ausgesandt" [20], ist die Taktvorzeichnung ein c. Aber bestimmt soll dieser Abschnitt nicht doppelt so langsam wie die beiden vorhergehenden sein. Angenommen, das Tempo soll unverändert bleiben, dann ist es möglich, „Doch eh' wir dieses tun" [22], dem eine **2** vorgezeichnet ist, in Wirklichkeit so zu nehmen, als ob ihm eine **1** voranstünde, was ein viel besseres Tempo ergäbe als das, was durch die **2** impliziert wird. Vielleicht hat der Kopist die Ebenen mit Absicht verschoben. In dieser Ausgabe sind die Taktvorzeichnungen der Tenbury-Handschrift vorgezogen worden.

Die einzige scheinbar unmögliche Taktvorzeichnung ist die **3** in „Unser Streben" [37]. Hier wird ein langsameres Tempo vorgeschlagen. Aber in der ganzen Ausgabe liegt der Nachdruck auf der Kontinuität der Partitur. Die Tenbury-Handschrift notiert zum Beispiel den Takt, der „Vernichtungsfreud' uns lacht" [38] und den *Hexentanz* [39], die beide eine **2** vorgezeichnet haben, verbindet, folgendermaßen: ♩ 𝅗𝅥 ‖ 𝅘𝅥𝅯 ♬♬

In dieser Ausgabe ist der Doppelstrich weggelassen worden wie so oft in der Tenbury-Handschrift an ähnlichen

Nahtstellen, etwa zwischen „Doch eh' wir dieses tun" [22] und „In der heimlichen Gruft" [23]. Ähnlich wird im *Hexentanz* der Wechsel von **3** zurück zu ¢ (oder **2**) so notiert: 3 ♩ 𝅗𝅥 ‖¢ ♪

In dieser Ausgabe erscheint er als: ¢ ♩ 𝅗𝅥 [𝄾] ♪

wobei Tempo (und Metrum) im letzten Takt der Tonfolge im **3**er-Takt wechseln. In einigen anderen Fällen ist ein Doppelstrich durch einen einfachen Taktstrich ersetzt worden (nach 2, 8, 10, 17, 19, 26, 31, 41), aber andere Veränderungen an der Notationsweise wurden nicht vorgenommen.

Die Bindebögen, dynamischen Bezeichnungen und Continuo-Bezifferung (eingerichtet entsprechend den Heute üblichen Tonart-Vorzeichnungen) in dieser Ausgabe gehen auf Lesarten der Quellen sowohl von Tenbury als auch Tatton Park zurück. In diesen Dingen stimmen die beiden Handschriften nicht überein, aber sie widersprechen sich auch nur selten. Die Tatton Park-Handschrift enthält zum Beispiel den Vermerk *leise* über dem Continuo-Auftakt zu „Doch eh' wir dieses tun" [22]. Die Tenbury-Handschrift gibt keine dynamische Bezeichnung, also auch keine widersprüchliche. Daher lassen sich die dynamischen Angaben beider Quellen leicht miteinander verbinden.

Bei der Verwendung von Bindebögen liegt es nicht in der Absicht dieser Ausgabe, in allen Fällen anzugleichen oder einem konsequenten Muster zu folgen, sondern die Unterschiede zu beachten. Daher werden nicht alle Melismen automatisch mit Bindebögen versehen. Die punktierten Melismen in „Oft an lieber Berge Stelle" [29] sind in keiner der beiden Quellen gebunden. Ganz ähnliche punktierte Passagen in „Unser Streben" [37] sind gebunden. Wenn man die Tempi der beiden Stücke betrachtet, scheint die An- oder Abwesenheit von Bindebögen eher auf Unterschiede in der rhythmischen Ausführung hinzudeuten. Im langsamen Tempo von „Oft an lieber Berge Stelle" (im c) mit seinen schreitenden Bässen sollten die punktierten Passagen sehr genau und möglicherweise überpunktiert sein. In dem sehr schnellen „Unser Streben" (im **3**) sollten dagegen die gebundenen punktierten Stellen höchstwahrscheinlich mehr als triolische denn als punktierte Gruppen ausgeführt werden. Deshalb ist in diesen Fällen die unterschiedliche Bindung eher als Hinweis auf die rhythmische Interpretation als auf die gebundene oder nicht gebundene Ausführung beibehalten worden.

Ähnlich wie „Unser Streben" steht auch der Chor „Euch Hügeln und Buchten" [14] im **3** und enthält ebenfalls viele punktierte Melismen. In der Tenbury-Handschrift sind nur die letzten zwei Noten dieser Passagen gebunden:

In der Tatton Park-Handschrift gilt die Bindung für die ganze Stelle. Die vorliegende Ausgabe folgt der Handschrift von Tatton Park. Das schnelle Tempo, in dem der Chor ausgeführt werden sollte, verwandelt, wie in „Unser Streben", die punktierten Figuren in Triolen. Man sollte sich diesen Satz vielleicht als Hochzeits-Gigue vorstellen. Nicht nur die Bindungen, sondern auch die widersprüchliche rhythmische Notierung der Auftakte (die so typisch ist für duolische Barockstücke, die nach triolischer Ausführung verlangen) zeigen den triolischen Rhythmus an. So steht in Takt 9 der Auftakt in allen Stimmen in gleichen Achteln. In Takt 20 indessen, bei der Wiederholung der Phrase, bestehen die Auftakte allesamt aus einem punktierten Achtel mit Sechzehntel, und in Takt 35 vermischen sich beide Versionen durch alle Stimmen und sogar in den verdoppelnden Instrumentalstimmen (II. Violine und Viola). Diese rhythmischen Inkonsequenzen wurden beibehalten als Hinweis auf die mutmaßliche Ausführung dieser Passagen im triolischen Rhythmus. Solche Widersprüche sind in der Partitur allerdings einmalig.

In dem Versuch, das schwierige Problem des Continuo auf praktische Weise zu lösen, bieten diese Begleitausgaben eine Reihe von Lösungen an. Der Klavierauszug enthält eine Stimme für Tasteninstrument, die teilweise eine Zusammenfassung der Streicherstimmen, und teilweise eine Aussetzung darstellt, wobei diese durchweg in kleinen Noten angegeben ist. Diese Klavierpartitur sollte daher besonders zum Lesen, Studieren und Proben geeignet sein. Obwohl die leihweise erhältliche Orchesterpartitur keine Aussetzung enthält, wurde die Bezifferung, die die der Tenbury- und der Tatton Park-Quelle vereinigt, durch editorische Bezifferungen in Klammern vermehrt. Der Herausgeber hofft, durch die Bereitstellung einer vollständigen Bezifferung zu einer improvisierenden Aussetzung anzuregen. Jedoch wurde den Einzelstimmen auch eine zusammengefaßte Partitur mit vollständiger Aussetzung des Continuo beigefügt, um Amateure und Schulgruppen nicht von einer Aufführung von *Dido* abzuhalten, Organisationen, denen diese Partitur so gute Dienste geleistet hat. Die veröffentlichten Orchesterpartituren enthalten nur die Bezifferung, die sich in der Tenbury- oder Tatton Park-Handschrift findet.

Die Continuo-Aussetzung beruht auf der Dents in folgender Weise: die Aussetzungen für die Lieder sind im wesentlichen die seinen, jene der deklamierten Abschnitte sind im wesentlichen neu, wobei dies auch für die Aussetzungen der Chöre und der Tänze gilt, die zum großen Teil von Dent nicht zur Verfügung gestellt wurden. In allen Solostücken waren melodische und dramatische Erwägungen von ausschlaggebender Bedeutung. In den Chören und Tänzen bieten die Aussetzungen in der Hauptsache regelmäßige rhythmische Metren durch einfache Harmonisierungen. Je nach der Größe der Halle können diese durch Verdoppelung von Stimmen oder Belebung des Satzes durch kürzere Noten verstärkt werden.

Zu einer eingehenderen Diskussion der Probleme, die im Vorwort und im Revisionsbericht aufgeworfen wurden, zur musikalischen Analyse, der literarischen Geschichte und Interpretation des Textes und zur Aufführungsgeschichte siehe das in Kürze erscheinende Buch des Herausgebers über *Dido und Aeneas* (Oxford University Press).

Die Sätze wurden vom Herausgeber numeriert; im Klavierauszug sind editorische Binde- und Haltebögen mit senkrechten Strichen versehen worden. Abgesehen von den Nummern sind alle anderen herausgeberischen Zusätze durch eckige Klammern angezeigt oder, bei den Halte- und Bindebögen, durch gestrichelte Linien.

Ellen T. Harris

Übersetzung Gudrun Budde
und Dorothee Eberhardt

DIDO AND AENEAS

Overture

Nahum Tate
(1652–1712)

Henry Purcell
(1659–1695)
edited by Edward J. Dent
and Ellen T. Harris

 Printed in Great Britain

OXFORD UNIVERSITY PRESS, MUSIC DEPARTMENT, WALTON STREET, OXFORD OX2 6DP

21
25
29
32
36
1.
2.

ACT I

[Part I, Scene 1]

Scene: The Palace. Enter Dido and Belinda, and Train.
Palast. Dido, Belinda und Gefolge.

2
18
CHORUS 2
brow. Ban - ish sor - row, ban - ish care, Grief should ne'er ap - proach the
sein. Fort mit Sor - gen, fort mit Leid, Schön-heit sei da - von be-
Ban - ish sor - row, ban - ish care, Grief should ne'er ap - proach the
Fort mit Sor - gen, fort mit Leid, Schön - heit sei da - von be-
Ban - ish sor - row, ban - ish care, Grief should ne'er ap - proach the
Fort mit Sor - gen, fort mit Leid, Schön-heit sei da - von be-
Ban - ish sor - row, ban - ish care, Grief should ne'er ap - proach the
Fort mit Sor - gen, fort mit Leid, Schön-heit sei da - von be-

5
fair. Ban-ish sor-row, ban - ish care, Grief should ne'er ap-proach, should ne'er ap-
- freit, Fort mit Sor-gen, fort mit Leid, Sei da - von be - freit, ja Schönheit
fair. Ban-ish, ban - ish care, ban - ish sorrow, Grief should ne'er, should ne'er ap-
- freit, Fort mit Leid, fort mit Leid, die Schönheit sei da-
fair. Ban -ish sor-row, ban - ish, ban-ish care, Grief should ne'er ap - proach, should ne'er ap-
- freit, Fort mit Sor-gen, fort mit Leid, Schön - heit, Schönheit sei da-
fair. Ban-ish sor - row, ban-ish, ban - ish care, Grief should ne'er ap-
- freit. Fort mit Sor - gen, fort mit Leid, Schön - heit sei da-

- proach the fair, grief should ne'er ap - proach the fair.
Sei be - freit, Schön - - heit sei da - von be - freit.
- proach the fair, grief should ne'er, should ne'er ap - proach the fair.
- von be - freit, Schönheit sei da - von, da - von be-freit.
8 - proach the fair, grief should ne'er, should ne'er ap - proach the fair.
- von be - freit, Schönheit sei da - von, da - von be - freit.
- proach the fair, grief should ne'er ap - proach the fair.
- von be - freit, Schön - heit sei da - von be-freit.
3
Slow [𝅗𝅥. = 𝅝]
DIDO
Ah, ah, ah! Be - lin - da, I am
Ah, ah, ah! Be - lin - da, mei - ne
7
prest, with tor - ment, ah, ah, ah! Be -
Qual, sa - gen muss ich, ah, ah, ah! Be -

12
-lin - da, I am prest, With tor - ment not to be con - fest.
-lin - da, mei - ne Qual, Sa - gen muss ich, muss ich Dir ein - mal.

18
Ah, ah, ah! Be - lin - da, I am prest, with
Ah, ah, ah! Be - lin - da, mei - ne Qual, sa - gen

24
tor - ment, ah, ah, ah! Be - lin - da, I am
muss ich, ah, ah, ah! Be - lin - da, mei - ne

30
prest, With tor - ment not to be con - fest.
Qual, Sa - gen muss ich, muss ich Dir ein - mal.

36
Peace and I are stran - gers grown, peace and
Frie - de ist schon längst mir fern, Frie - de
41
I are stran - gers, stran - gers grown. I lan -
ist schon längst mir, längst mir fern. Mein Kum -
46
guish till my grief is known, I lan -
mer al - le Welt soll lern,' mein Kum -
51
guish till my grief is known, Yet
mer al - le Welt soll lern,' Doch

56
would not, yet would not, would not have it guess'd.
ra-ten, doch ra-ten, ra - ten soll sie ihn nicht.
61
Peace and I are stran - gers
Frie - de ist schon längst mir
67
Ritorn[elle]
grown, peace and I are stran - gers, stran - gers grown.
fern, Frie - de ist schon längst mir, längst mir fern.
73

79
4
BELINDA
Grief in-creas-es by con - ceal - ing.
Leid wird gröss-er in der Stil - le.
DIDO
Mine admits of no re - veal - ing.
Da - her meines Kummers Fül - le.
BELINDA
Then let me speak —
So hör mir zu:
4
the Tro - jan guest In - to your ten - der thoughts has prest. The
dem Gast aus Tro - ja ganz ge - weiht den Sinn Du hast. Zum
SECOND WOMAN
great - est bless - ing
gröss - ten Glück Ge -
7
Fate can give, Our Car - thage to se - cure, and Troy re - vive. The great - est
- schick uns lenkt, Kar - tha - go gleich wie Tro - ja neu ge - schenkt. Zum gröss - ten

5
CHORUS
11
blessing — Fate can give, Our Carthage to secure, and Troy — revive. When
Glück Geschick uns lenkt, Karthago gleich wie — Troja neu — geschenkt. Wenn
[𝅗𝅥. = 𝅗𝅥]
monarchs unite, how happy their state, They triumph at once o'er their
Herrscher vereint, wie gross ist ihr Glück, Sie lachen zugleich über
7
foes and their fate, they triumph, they triumph at once o'er their foes and their fate.
Feind und Geschick, sie lachen, sie lachen zugleich über Feind und Geschick.

6
DIDO
Whence could so much vir - tue spring, What storms, what battles did he
Von tapfren Ahnen er ent - sprang, Von Sturm, von Schlacht-en tönt sein
4
sing. Anchis-es' va - - lour mix'd with Ve - nus' charms, How soft, how
Sang! Anchis-es' Stär - - ke mit der Ve - nus Mild', Wie sanft, wie
7
soft in peace, and yet how fierce, how fierce in arms.
sanft als Freund, und doch wie hart in sei - ner Waf - fen - schild!
BELINDA
A tale so
Ein star - kes
10
strong and full of woe, Might melt the rocks as well as you.
Lied, so vol-ler Schmerz, Er - greift die Stei - ne wie Dein Herz.
SECOND WOMAN
What
Kein

DIDO
stubborn heart un-moved could see, Such distress, such pi - e-ty. Mine with
hart Gemüt er blik-ket ohn' Ge- winn, Sol-ches Leid, solch from-men Sinn. Da mich
storms of care opprest, Is taught to pi - ty the dis-
Leid und Sor - ge be-rührt, Hat mich das Mit - leid stets ge-
- trest. Mean wretch-es' grief can touch, So soft, so sen - si-ble my
- führt. Auch Ar - mer Leid ich fühl', So sanft, Empfin - dung ihm ge-
breast, But ah, but ah! I fear, I pi-ty his too much.
- bührt: Doch ach! doch ach! ich fürcht', mein Mitleid ist zu - viel.

7
BELINDA
SECOND WOMAN
Fear no dan - ger to en - sue, The he-ro loves as well as you.
Fürcht' nicht, dass Ge - fahr er - schien, Dein Held liebt Dich so wie Du ihn.
9
Ev - er gen - tle, ev - er smil - ing, And the cares of life be - guil - ing,
Vol - ler Froh - sinn, im - mer hei - ter, Kümmern Sor - gen ihn nicht wei - ter,
17
Fear no dan - ger to en - sue, The he - ro loves as well as you.
Fürcht' nicht, dass Ge - fahr er - schien, Dein Held liebt Dich so wie Du ihn.
25
[tr]
[tr]
Cu - pid strew your path with flowers, Ga-ther'd from E - ly - sian bowers.
A - mor streut den Pfad mit Blü - ten, Die sie im E - ly - sium hü - ten.

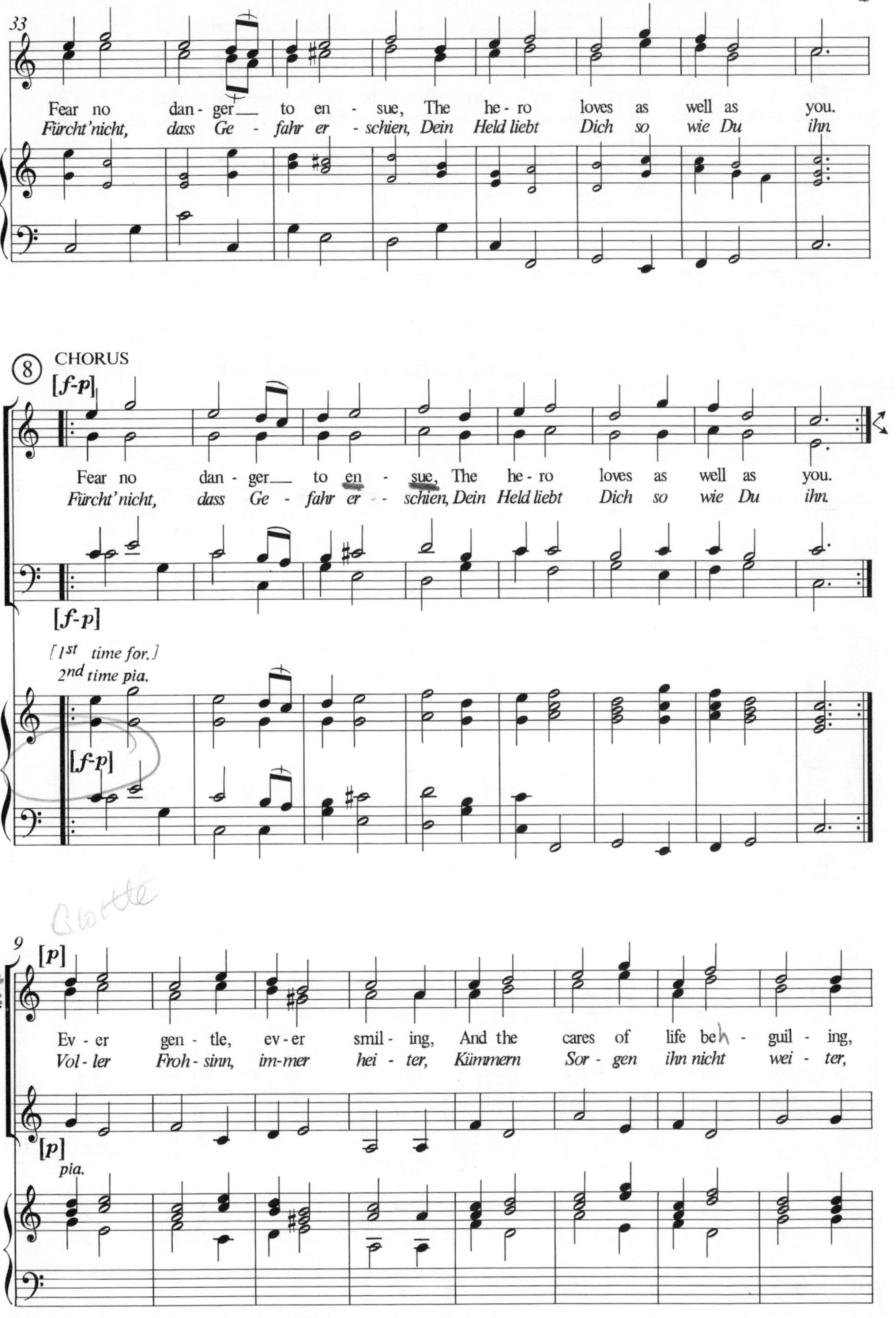

(8) CHORUS

[f-p]

Fear no dan - ger__ to en - sue, The he - ro loves as well as you.

Fürcht' nicht, dass Ge - fahr er - schien, Dein Held liebt Dich so wie Du ihn.

[f-p]

[1st time for.]
2nd time pia.

[f-p]

9

[p]

S. 1. 2.

Ev - er gen - tle, ev - er smil - ing, And the cares of life be - guil - ing,

Vol - ler Froh - sinn, im - mer hei - ter, Kümmern Sor - gen ihn nicht wei - ter,

A.

[p]

pia.

Dance this Cho[rus]. The Baske.[1]
Tanzen während des Gesangs. Baskische Tanz.

[1] See Editorial Notes

Aeneas enters with his train.
Aeneas tritt ein mit seinem Gefolge.

10
CHORUS
Cu - pid on - ly throws the dart, That's dread-ful, dread - ful, dread - ful,
A - mor ein - zig wirft den Pfeil, Der töd - lich, töd - lich, töd - lich,
Cu - pid on - ly throws the dart, That's dread - ful, dread - ful,
A - mor ein - zig wirft den Pfeil, Der töd - lich, töd - lich,
Cu - pid on - ly throws the dart,
A - mor ein - zig wirft den Pfeil,
Cu - pid on - ly
A - mor ein - zig
5
Cu - pid on - ly throws the dart, That's dread-ful to a war - rior's heart, that's
A - mor ein - zig wirft den Pfeil, Der töd- lich für des Krieg - ers Heil, der
dread - ful, Cu - pid on - ly throws the dart, on - ly throws the dart, That's
töd - lich, A - mor ein - zig wirft den Pfeil, ein - zig wirft den Pfeil, Der
Cu - pid on - ly throws the dart, That's
A - mor ein - zig wirft den Pfeil, Der
throws the dart, That's dread - ful, dread - ful, Cu - pid on - ly throws the dart, That's
wirft den Pfeil, Der töd - lich, töd - lich, A - mor ein - zig wirft den Pfeil, Der

9
dread - ful to a war - rior's heart. And she that wounds, and she that wounds can
töd - lich für des Krieg - ers Heil. Und nur die Lieb,' und nur die Lieb', nur
dread - ful to—— a war - rior's heart. And she that wounds, and she that wounds can
töd - lich für—— des Krieg - ers Heil. Und nur die Lieb,' und nur die Lieb', nur
dread - ful to a war - rior's heart. And she that wounds, and she that wounds can
töd - lich für des Krieg - ers Heil. Und nur die Lieb,' und nur die Lieb', nur
dread - ful to a war - rior's heart. And she that wounds, and she that wounds can
töd - lich für des Krieg - ers Heil. Und nur die Lieb,' und nur die Lieb', nur

13
on - ly,— on - ly cure— the smart, can on - ly,— on - ly cure the smart.
Sie kann— trös - ten mich— in Eil', nur Sie— kann— trös - ten mich in Eil'.
on - ly, on - ly cure the smart, can on - ly, on - ly cure the smart.
Sie— kann trös - ten mich in Eil', nur Sie kann trös - ten mich in Eil'.
on - ly, on - ly cure the smart, can on - ly, on - ly cure the smart.
Sie kann trös - ten mich in Eil', nur Sie kann trös - ten mich in Eil'.
on - ly, on - ly cure the smart, can on - ly, on - ly cure the smart.
Sie kann trös - ten mich in Eil', nur Sie kann trös - ten mich in Eil'.

11
AENEAS
If not for mine, for Em-pire's sake, Some pi - ty on your
Ist's nicht für mich, sei's für Dein Reich, Dem Lie - ben - den Dein
3
lov - er take. Ah, ah! make not in a hope - less fire, A he - ro
Herz er - weich'! Oh, oh! lass mich nicht im Feu - er stehn, Ohn' Hoffnungs-
6
fall, and Troy once more ex - pire.
- strahl, und wie - der Tro-ja un - ter - gehn.
12 Quick
go to Tim
BELINDA
soft
Pur - sue thy con-quest, Love, pur -
Die Lie - be hat ge-siegt, die
Quick
3
loud
- sue thy con-quest, Love, pur - sue, pur-sue, pur - sue thy con-quest, pur -
Lie - be hat ge-siegt, sie hat ge-siegt, ja, ja, die Lie - be, die

6
soft
loud
-sue thy—con-quest, Love. Pur - sue thy con-quest, Love, pur - sue thy con-quest, Love, pur -
Lie-be—hat—ge-siegt. Die Lie-be hat ge-siegt, die Lie-be hat ge-siegt, sie
9
sue, pur-sue, ——— pur - sue thy conquest, pur - sue thy—con-quest, Love. Her
hat ge-siegt, ——— ja, ja, die Lie-be, die Lie-be—hat—ge - siegt. Sie
12
eyes Con-fess the flame, her eyes con-fess the flame her tongue de - nies. Her eyes Con-fess the
blickt Das Feu-er selbst, sie blickt das Feu-er, das ihr Wort—er - stickt. Sie blickt Das Feu-er
15
flame, her eyes con-fess the flame ——— her tongue de - nies. Pur-sue thy con-quest,
selbst, sie blickt das Feu-er, das ——— ihr Wort—er - stickt. Die Lie-be hat ge -

² See Appendix and Editorial Notes

7
groves, and the cool sha - dy foun - tains, Let the tri - - - umphs, let the
Schluchten, Euch Quel - len im Schat - ten, Sei die Freu - - - de, sei die
groves, and the cool sha - dy foun - tains, Let the tri - umphs, the tri - -
Schluchten, Euch Quel - len im Schat - ten, Sei die Freu - de, die Freu - -
groves, and the cool sha - dy foun - tains, Let the tri - - - umphs, let the
Schluchten, Euch Quel - len im Schat - ten, Sei die Freu - - - de, sei die
groves, and the cool sha - dy foun - tains, Let the tri - umphs, let the tri - umphs, the
Schluchten, Euch Quel - len im Schat - ten, Sei die Freu - de, sei die Freu - de, die
12
tri - - - umphs of Love and of Beau - ty be shown.
Freu - - - de an Lie - be und Schön-heit ge - zeigt.
- umphs, the tri-umphs of Love and of Beau - ty be shown.
- de, die Freu - de an Lie - be und Schön- heit ge - zeigt.
tri - umphs, the tri-umphs of Love and of Beau - ty be - shown.
Freu - de, die Freu - de an Lie - be und Schön- heit ge - zeigt.
tri - - - umphs of Love and of Beau - ty be - shown.
Freu - - - de an Lie - be und Schön-heit ge - zeigt.

18
Let the tri - - - umphs, let the
Sei die Freu - - - de, sei die
Let the tri - umphs, the tri - -
Sei die Freu - de, die Freu - -
Let the tri- - - umphs, let the
Sei die Freu - - - de, sei die
Let the tri - umphs, let the tri - umphs, the
Sei die Freu - de, sei die Freu - de, die
23
tri - - - umphs of Love and of Beau - ty be shown. To the hills and the
Freu - - - de an Lie - be und Schönheit ge - zeigt. Euch Hü - geln und
- umphs, the tri - umphs of Love and of Beau - ty be shown. To the hills and the
- de, die Freu - de an Lie - be und Schönheit ge - zeigt. Euch Hü - geln und
tri - umphs, the tri - umphs of Love and of Beau - ty be shown. To the hills and the
Freu - de, die Freu - de an Lie - be und Schönheit ge - zeigt. Euch Hü - geln und
tri - - - umphs of Love and of Beau - ty be shown. To the hills and the
Freu - - - de an Lie - be und Schönheit ge - zeigt. Euch Hü - geln und

29

vales, to the rocks and the mountains, To the musical— groves, and the cool shady
Buchten, Euch— Fel-sen und Mat-ten, Euch— sang-reich-en— Schluchten, Euch Quel-len im

vales, to the rocks and the mountains, To the mu-si-cal groves, and the cool sha-dy
Buchten, Euch— Fel-sen und Mat-ten, Euch— sang-reich-en Schluchten, Euch Quel-len im

vales, to the rocks and the mountains, To the mu-si-cal groves, and the cool sha-dy
Buchten, Euch— Fel-sen und Mat-ten, Euch— sang-reich-en Schluchten, Euch— Quel-len im

vales, to the rocks and the mountains, To the mu-si-cal groves, and the cool sha-dy
Buchten, Euch— Fel-sen und Mat-ten, Euch— sang-reich-en Schluchten, Euch Quel-len im

35

foun-tains, Let the tri- - - -umphs, let the tri- - - -umphs of
Schat-ten, Sei die Freu- - - -de, sei die Freu- - - -de an

foun-tains, Let the tri-umphs, the tri- - - -umphs, the tri-umphs of
Schat-ten, Sei die Freu-de, die Freu- - - -de, die Freu-de an

foun-tains, Let the tri- - - -umphs, let the tri-umphs, the tri-umphs of
Schat-ten, Sei die Freu- - - -de, sei die Freu-de, die Freu-de an

foun-tains, Let the tri-umphs, let the tri-umphs, the tri- - - -umphs of
Schat-ten, Sei die Freu-de, sei die Freu-de, die Freu- - - -de an

40
Love and of Beau - ty be shown. Go re - vel, ye Cu - pids, go
Lie - be und Schön-heit ge - zeigt. Nun schwärmt, A - mo - ret - ten, nun
Love and of Beau - ty be shown. Go re - vel, ye
Lie - be und Schön-heit ge - - zeigt. Nun schwärmt, A - mo -
Love and of. Beau - ty be shown. Go re - vel, ye Cu-pids, go re - vel, go
Lie - be und Schön-heit ge - zeigt. Nun schwärmt, A - mo - ret - ten, nun schwär-met, nun
Love and of Beau - ty be shown. Go re - vel, go re - vel, ye Cu - pids, go
Lie - be und Schön- heit ge - zeigt. Nun schwärmt, A - mo - ret - ten, nun schwär-met, nun

46
re - vel, go re - vel, ye Cu - pids, go re - vel, the day is your own.
schwär - met, nun schwärmt, A - mo - ret - ten, nun schwär - met, und bleibt uns ge - neigt.
Cu - pids, go re - vel, go re - vel, ye Cu - pids, the day is your own.
- ret - ten, nun schwär - met, nun schwärmt, A - mo - ret - ten, und bleibt uns ge - neigt.
re - vel, ye Cu - pids, go re - vel, ye Cu - pids, the day is your own.
schwärmt, A - mo - ret - ten, nun schwärmt, A - mo - ret - ten, und bleibt uns ge - neigt.
re - vel, go re - vel, go re - vel, ye Cu - pids, the day is your own.
schwär - met, nun schwär - met, nun schwärmt, A - mo - ret - ten, und bleibt uns ge - neigt.

The Triumphing Dance
Siegestanz

(At the End of the Dance Thunder and Light'ning)[3]
(Zum Schluss des Tanzes Donner und Blitzen)

Act II. Scene 1

[Part I, Scene 2]

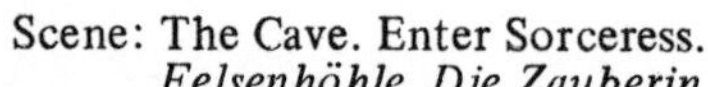

Scene: The Cave. Enter Sorceress.
Felsenhöhle. Die Zauberin.

(Prelude for the Witches)
(Präludium für die Hexen)

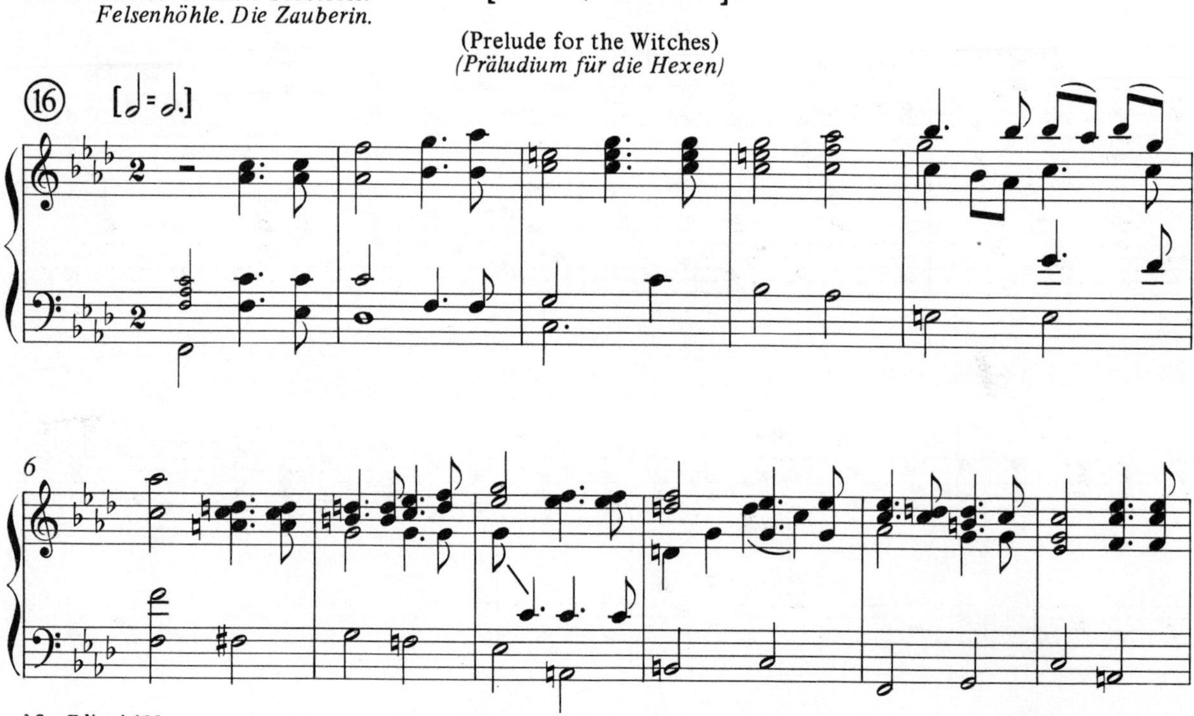

[3] See Editorial Notes

12
tr
17
SORCERESS
Way-ward sis-ters, you that fright, The lone - ly tra-vel - ler by
Düst'-re Schwestern, Schreck-ge - stalt! Ihr quält den Einsam- en im
Play Soft
21
night, Who like dis - mal ra - vens cry - ing, Beat the win - dows of the
Wald. Fliegt an Un - glücks-tod - es - stät - te Ra - ben - gleich ums Ster - be -
25
dy - ing, Ap - pear, ap-pear at my call, and share in the fame Of a
bet - te. Er - scheint, erscheint mei-nem Ruf, dann teilt Ihr den Ruhm, Und ver -

29
mis - chief shall make all Car - thage flame. Ap - pear, ap -
- bren - net die Stadt, Di - dos Kö - nig - tum Er-scheint, er -
33
Enter Inchantresses (Witches)
Die Hexen
FIRST WITCH
- pear, ap - pear, ap - pear!
- scheint, erscheint, er - scheint!
Say, bel - dam, say, what's thy will?
Sag, Al - te, sag, was soll'n wir tun?
17
CHORUS
Harm's our de - light and mis - chief all our skill, harm's our de - light and
Tod un - ser Glück, kein Un - heil lässt uns ruhn, Tod un - ser Glück, kein
Harm's our de - light and mis - chief all our skill, harm's our de - light
Tod un - ser Glück, kein Un - heil lässt uns ruhn, Tod un - ser Glück,
Harm's our de - light and mis - chief all our skill, harm's our de - light and
Tod un - ser Glück, kein Un - heil lässt uns ruhn, Tod un - ser Glück, kein
Harm's our de - light and mis - chief all our skill, harm's our de - light
Tod un - ser Glück, kein Un - heil lässt uns ruhn, Tod un - ser Glück,

mis - chief all our skill, and mis - chief, mis - chief all our skill.
Un - heil lässt uns ruhn, kein Un - heil, Un - heil lässt uns ruhn.
and mis - chief all our skill, and mis - chief, mis - chief all our skill.
kein Un - heil lässt uns ruhn, kein Un - heil, Un - heil lässt uns ruhn.
mis - chief all our skill, and mis - chief, mis - chief, mis - chief all our skill.
Un - heil lässt uns ruhn, kein Un - heil, Un - heil, Un - heil lässt uns ruhn.
and mis - chief all our skill, and mis - chief all our skill.
kein Un - heil lässt uns ruhn, kein Un - heil lässt uns ruhn.
18
SORCERESS
The Queen of Car - thage, whom we hate, As we do
Kar - tha - gos Her - rin, sehr ver - hasst, Wie al - le
all in pros - p'rous state, Ere sun - set shall most
Fro - hen uns zur Last, Vor A - bend nichts ihr

7
wretch - ed prove, De-priv'd of fame, of life, and
ü - brig blieb, Zerstört ihr Ruhm, ihr Le - ben, ih - re
19
[♩. = ♩]
CHORUS
love. Ho ho ho ho ho ho ho ho ho ho ho ho ho ho ho ho ho ho
Lieb'!
7
ho ho ho ho ho ho ho ho ho ho ho ho ho ho ho

12
ho ho ho ho ho ho ho ho ho ho ho ho ho!

20
FIRST WITCH
SECOND WITCH
Ru - in'd ere the set of sun? Tell us, tell us, tell us,
Heut' schon, eh' die Son - ne sinkt? Sag uns, sag uns, sag uns,

3
SORCERESS
tell us, how shall this be done? The Tro - jan Prince you know is bound By
sag uns, wie uns das ge - lingt. Ae - ne - as wur - de aus - ge - sandt Vom
Play Soft
[Soft]

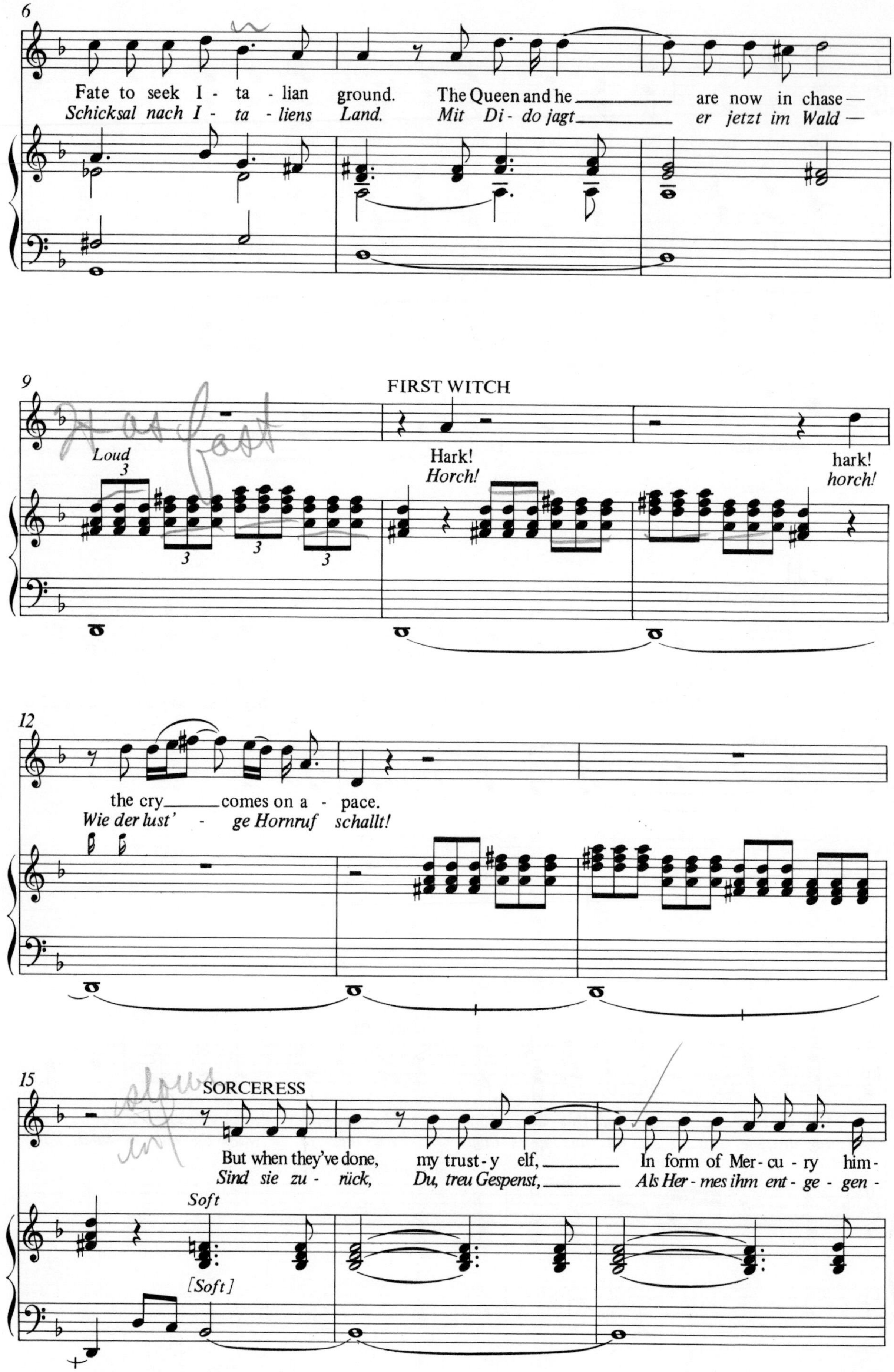

9

FIRST WITCH

Loud

Hark! hark!

Horch! horch!

12

the cry comes on a - pace.

Wie der lust' - ge Hornruf schallt!

15

SORCERESS

But when they've done, my trust-y elf, In form of Mer-cu-ry him-

Sind sie zu - rück, Du, treu Gespenst, Als Her - mes ihm ent - ge - gen -

Soft

[Soft]

18
- self, As sent from Jove shall chide his stay, And
- rennst, Von Zeus ge - sandt, triffst Du ihn dort, Und
20
charge him sail to-night with all his fleet a - way
schickst ihn a - bends mit der gan - zen Flot - te
21
CHORUS
- way. Ho ho ho ho ho ho ho ho ho ho ho ho ho ho
fort.

4 See Editorial Notes

5
storm. But ere we this per - form, But
nun. Doch eh' wir die - ses tun, Doch
But ere we this per - form, We'll con - jure for a
Doch eh' wir die - ses tun, Er - heb' sich Sturmwind
9
ere we this per - form, We'll con - jure for a storm, we'll
eh' wir die - ses tun, Er - heb' sich Sturmwind nun, er -
storm, we'll con - - -
nun, er - heb'
13
1. 2.
con - jure for a storm. storm. To mar their hunt - ing
- heb' sich Sturmwind nun. nun. Ver - der - bet ih - ren
- jure for a storm. But storm. To
sich Sturmwind nun. Doch nun. Ver -

16
sport, to mar their hunt - ing sport, And drive
Sport, ver - der - bet ih - ren Sport, Und trei - - -
mar their hunt - ing mar their hunt - ing sport, And drive
- der - bet ih - ren Sport, ja, ih - ren Sport, Und trei - - - - -
20
'em back to
- - - - - - bet sie nach Hau - se
'em back to
- - - - - - bet sie nach Hau - se
24
court, and drive
fort, und trei - - - - - - - - -
court, and drive
fort, und trei - - - - - - -

28
'em, drive 'em back to court. To court.
bet sie nach Hau - se fort. Ver - fort.
'em, drive 'em back to court. court.
bet sie nach Hau - se fort. fort.
1.
2.
23
CHORUS (in a Manner of an Echo)
(wie ein Echo)
[Loud]
Soft
Loud
In our deep vault-ed cell, -ed cell, the charm we'll pre - pare, pre - pare, Too
In der heim-li-chen Gruft, -chen Gruft, das Werk sei voll - bracht, voll - bracht, Zu
7
dread - ful a prac - tice, too dread - ful a prac - tice, too dread - ful, too
schreck - lich vol - len - den, zu schreck - lich vol - len - den, zu schreck - lich, zu

12
Loud
Soft
Loud
Soft
dread - ful, a prac - tice, a prac - tice, for this o - pen air, for
schreck - lich, vol - len - den, vol - len - den, für son - ni - ge Luft, für
Loud
Soft
Loud
Soft
Loud
Soft
Loud
Soft
17
Loud
Soft
Loud
this o - pen air. In our deep vault - ed cell, - ed cell, the
son - ni - ge Luft. In der heim - lich - en Gruft, - chen Gruft, das
Loud
Soft
Loud
Loud
Soft
Loud
22
Soft
Loud
Soft
charm we'll pre - pare, pre - pare, Too dread - ful a prac - tice, too dread - ful a
Werk sei voll - bracht, voll - bracht, Zu schrecklich vol - len - den, zu schrecklich vol -
Soft
Loud
Soft
Soft
Loud
Soft

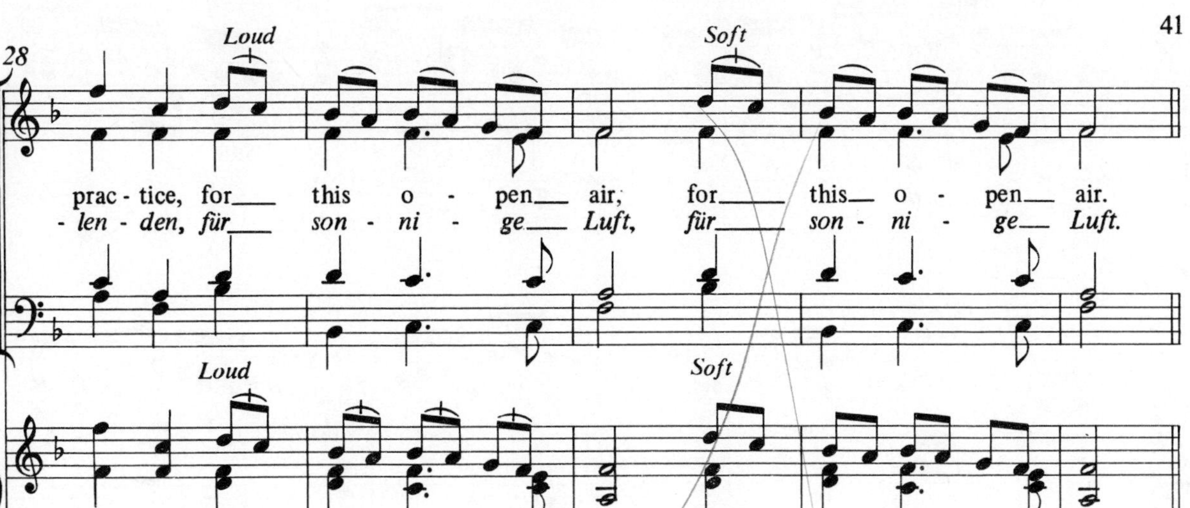

Eccho Dance. Inchantresses and Fairies

Echotanz. Hexen und Feen

(Echo Dance of Furies)

(Echotanz der Furien)

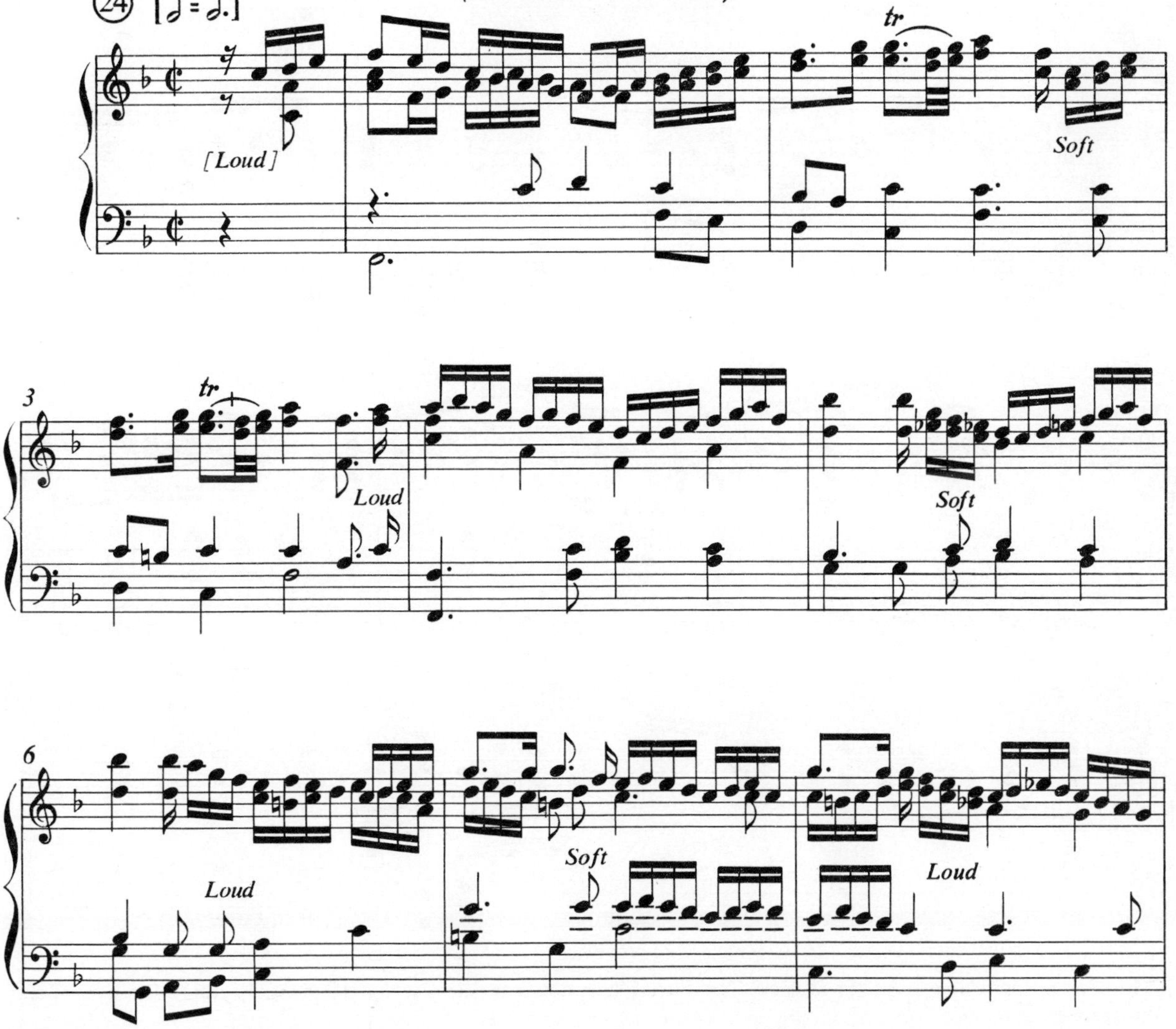

24 [𝅗𝅥 = 𝅗𝅥.]

[Loud] Soft

3 Loud Soft

6 Loud Soft Loud

(Thunder & Light'ning[,] horrid Musick. The Furies sink down in the Cave[,] the Rest fly up[.] The End of the first part.)[5]

(Donner und Blitzen. Schreckliche Musik. Die Furien versinken in der Felsenhöhle. Die übrigen fliegen auf. Ende des ersten Teils.)

[5]See Editorial Notes

Act II. Scene 2

[Part II, Scene 1]

Scene: The Grove. Enter Aeneas, Dido and Belinda, and their Train.[6]
Die Schlucht. Aeneas, Dido, Belinda und Gefolge.

[6] See Editorial Notes

9
So fair the game, so rich the sport, Di -
So schön die Jagd, Beu - te zu - gleich, Di -
[2nd time]

13
- a - na's self might to these woods re - sort.
- a - na selbst hat wohl hier ihr Be - reich.

17
So fair the game, so rich the sport, Di -
So schön die Jagd, Beu - te zu - gleich, Di -

21
1.
2.
- a - na's self might to these woods re - sort. - sort.
- a - na selbst hat wohl hier ihr Be - reich. - reich.

(27) CHORUS

Thanks to these lone - some, lone-some vales, These de - sert, de - sert
Dank Dir, Du Ein-sam - keit, Ein - sam - keit, Tä - ler und Hü - gel ver -

Thanks to these lone - some, lone-some vales, These de - sert, de - sert
Dank Dir, Du Einsam - keit, Ein - sam - keit, Tä - ler und Hü - gel ver -

Thanks to these lone - some, lone-some vales, These de - sert, de - sert
Dank Dir, Du Ein - sam - keit, Ein - sam - keit, Tä - ler und Hü - gel ver -

Thanks to these lone - some, lone-some vales, These de - sert, de - sert
Dank Dir, Du Ein - sam - keit, Ein - sam - keit, Tä - ler und Hü-gel ver -

7

hills and dales. So fair the game, so rich the sport, Di -
- las - sen so weit. So schön die Jagd, Beu - te zu - gleich, Di -

hills and dales. So fair the game, so rich the
- las - sen so weit. So schön die Jagd, Beu - te zu -

hills and dales. So fair the game, so rich the sport, Di -
- las - sen so weit. So schön die Jagd, Beu - te zu - gleich, Di -

hills and dales. So fair the game, so rich the
- las - sen so weit. So schön die Jagd, Beu - te zu -

(28) Gitter ground a Dance[7]

Gitarrentanz. (Chaconne).

[7] See Appendix and Editorial Notes

29
SECOND WOMAN
Oft she vi - sits this loved moun - tain, Oft she bathes her in this foun - tain,
Oft an lie - ber Ber - ge Stel - le, Oft be - sucht sie die - se Quel - le,
Oft she vi - sits this loved moun - tain, Oft she bathes her in this foun - tain.
Oft an lie - ber Ber - ge Stel - le, Oft be - sucht sie die - se Quel - le.
Here, here Ac - tae - on met his fate, here, here Ac -
Hier, hier Ak - tä - on ging zu Grund, hier, hier Ak -

17
- tae - on met his fate, Pur-sued by
- tä - on ging zu Grund, Es ris - - - - sen ihn
20
his own hounds. And af - ter, af - ter mor - tal wounds, and
sei - ne Hun - de. Und end - lich nach der Tod - es - wun - de, und
23
af - ter, af - - - ter mor - tal wounds, Dis- cov- -
end - lich nach der Tod - es - wun - de, Zu spät
26
- - er'd too, too late, And af - ter, af - ter mor - -
war's für den Fund, Und end - lich nach der Tod

29
- - tal wounds, Dis - cov - er'd too, too late, Here Ac -
- - eswun - de, Zu spät war's für den Fund, Hier Ak -
32
A dance to entertain Aeneas by Dido's Women
Tanz der Frauen Didos vor Aeneas
- tae - on met his fate.
- tä - on ging zu Grund.
Ritorn[elle]
35
39
43
tr

tr
30
AENEAS
Be-hold, upon my bending spear, A monster's head stands
Sieh hier auf starkem Lanzenschaft, Den Eberkopf im
bleeding, With tushes far exceeding, Those did Venus' huntsman
Blute, Er übertraf an Mutte, Den einst Venus hinge-

[Quick]
DIDO
tear. The skies are cloud - ed. Hark, hark, how thun -
rafft. Welch' Wolken-him - mel! Horch! horch! Das Grol -
Violin
- der Rends the mountain oaks a - sun-der.
- len Lässt der Ei - chen Wip-fel rol -len!
Violins
BELINDA
31
[Quick]
Haste, haste to town, haste, haste, haste, haste, haste to town, haste, haste, haste,
Schnell, schnell zur Stadt, schnell, schnell, schnell, schnell, schnell zur Stadt, schnell, schnell, schnell,
haste, this o-pen field, No shel - ter, this o-pen field, no shel - ter from the storm,
schnell, das off'ne Feld Kein Schutzdach, das off'ne Feld kein Schutzdach ge - gen Sturm,

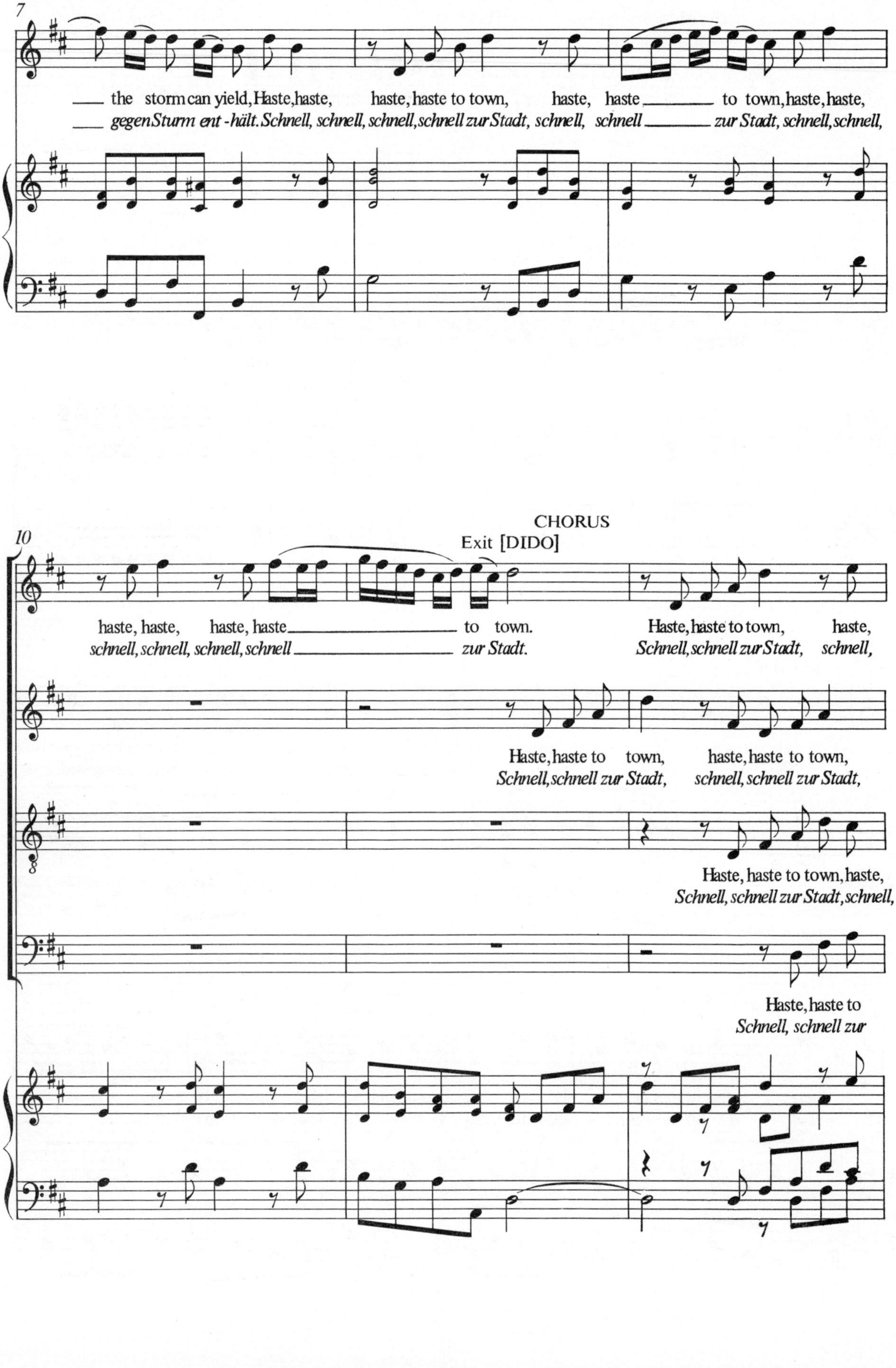

10

CHORUS

Exit [DIDO]

haste, haste, haste, haste — to town. Haste, haste to town, haste,
schnell, schnell, schnell, schnell — zur Stadt. Schnell, schnell zur Stadt, schnell,

Haste, haste to town, haste, haste to town,
Schnell, schnell zur Stadt, schnell, schnell zur Stadt,

Haste, haste to town, haste,
Schnell, schnell zur Stadt, schnell,

Haste, haste to
Schnell, schnell zur

13
haste, haste, haste, haste to town, haste, haste, haste,
schnell, schnell, schnell, schnell zur Stadt, schnell, schnell, schnell,
haste, haste to town, haste, haste, haste, haste to town, haste,
schnell, schnell zur Stadt, schnell, schnell, schnell, schnell zur Stadt, schnell,
haste, haste, haste, haste to town, haste,
schnell, schnell, schnell, schnell zur Stadt, schnell,
town, haste, haste, haste, haste, haste, haste to town,
Stadt, schnell, schnell, schnell, schnell, schnell, schnell zur Stadt,
15
haste, this o - pen field, No shel - ter, this o - pen field, no
schnell, das off - 'ne Feld Kein Schutz - dach, das off - 'ne Feld kein
haste to town, haste, haste, this o - pen field, No shel - ter, this
schnell zur Stadt, schnell, schnell, das off - 'ne Feld Kein Schutz-dach, das
haste, haste, haste, this o - pen field, No shel - ter, this o - pen field, no
schnell zur Stadt, das off - 'ne Feld Kein Schutz-dach, das off - 'ne Feld kein
haste, haste to town, this o - pen field, No shel - ter, this
schnell, schnell zur Stadt, das off - 'ne Feld Kein Schutz - dach, das

17
shel - ter from the storm, the storm can yield. Haste, haste,
Schutz - dach ge - gen Sturm, ge-gen Sturm ent - hält. Schnell, schnell,
o - pen field, no shel - ter from the storm, the storm can yield. Haste, haste to
off - 'ne Feld kein Schutz - dach ge - gen Sturm, den Sturm ent - hält. Schnell, schnell zur
shel - ter from the storm, the storm can yield. Haste,
Schutz - dach ge - gen Sturm, den Sturm ent - hält. Schnell,
o - pen field, no shel - ter from the storm can yield. Haste,
off - 'ne Feld kein Schutz - dach ge - gen Sturm ent - hält. Schnell,
19
haste, haste to town, haste, haste to town, haste, haste,
schnell, schnell zur Stadt, schnell, schnell zur Stadt, schnell, schnell,
town, haste, haste, haste, haste to town, haste, haste to town, haste, haste, haste,
Stadt, schnell, schnell, schnell, schnell zur Stadt, schnell, schnell zur Stadt, schnell, schnell zur
haste, haste, haste to town, haste, haste to town, haste, haste,
schnell, schnell, schnell zur Stadt, schnell, schnell zur Stadt, schnell, schnell,
haste, haste, haste to town, haste, haste, haste,
schnell, schnell, schnell zur Stadt, schnell, schnell, schnell,

The Spirit of the Sorceress descends to Aeneas in likeness of Mercury.
Das Gespenst der Zauberinnen herabsteigt vor Aeneas in der Gestalt des Merkurys.

8 See Editorial Notes

7
stay. Jove com - mands thee waste no more In love's de - lights, those
mehr. Zeus ver - bie - tet Dir für Lie - be - lei die Zeit zu
9
pre - cious hours, Al - low'd by th'Almighty pow'rs To gain
nüt - zen ganz, Die gab die all-mächt'ge Kraft Zur Fahrt
tr
11
AENEAS
th'He - spe - rian shore, And ru - in'd Troy re - store. Jove's com -
nach La - tiums Strand, Zer - stör - ten Tro - jas Pfand. Zeus' Be -
13
Spirit vanishes.
Gespenst verschwindet.
- mands shall be o - bey'd, To - night our an - chors shall be weigh'd. But ah!
- feh - len gilt mein Le-ben, Heut' Nacht lasst uns die An - ker he - ben. Doch oh!
[colla voce]

16
but ah! what lan - guage can I
doch oh! Fänd Trös - tung ich da -
19
try, My in - jur'd Queen to pa - ci-fy. No sooner she re-signs her
- zu, Wie bring die Kön'-gin ich zur Ruh? Nicht länger sie verschliesst ihr
22
heart, But from her arms I'm forc'd to part. How can so hard a fate be
Herz, Doch von ihr reisst mich Trennungsschmerz: Wie grausam kannst Du, Schick-sal,
25
took, One night en - joy'd, the next for - sook. Yours be the
sein? Nach schönster Nacht ist man al - lein! Ihr Göt-ter,

28

blame ye gods, for I O - bey your — will, but with more — ease — could —

habt die Schuld, denn ich Ge - hor - che — Euch, doch viel lie - ber stürb ich sicher -

31

die, but with more, more — ease — could die.

- lich, doch viel lie - ber stürb — ich — si - cher - lich.

[(33) Ritornelle (25) again
Wieder Ritornello (25)][9] (The End of the 2d Act)

Act III

[Part II, Scene 2]

Scene: The Ships. Enter the Sailors.[10] The Sorceress and her Inchantresses.[11]
Die Schiffe. Matrosen. Zauberin und Hexen.

(34) (Prelude)

9, 10, 11 See Editorial Notes

13

19

24

30

36 FIRST SAILOR

Come a - way, fel - low sail - ors, come a - way, your an - chors be

Kommt an Bord, ihr Ma - tro - sen, kommt an Bord, die An - ker wir

41
weigh - ing, Time and tide will ad - mit no de - lay - ing. Take a
hie - ven, Zeit und Flut lässt uns län - ger nicht blie - wen; Sagt ver -

45
booz - y short leave of your nymphs on the shore, And si - lence their
- dammt kurz Leb - wohl Eu - ren Nym - phen am Land, Um - fasst ih - re

50
mourn - ing With vows of re - turn - ing, But nev - er in - tend - ing to
Mie - der, Ver - sprecht ihr kommt wie - der, Auch wenn Ihr nie wie - der - seht

55
vis - it them more, no, nev-er in - tend-ing to vis - it them
hier die - sen Strand, auch wenn Ihr nie wie-der - seht hier die - sen

60
more, no, nev - er, no, nev-er in - tend - ing to vis - it them
Strand, auch wenn ihr nie wie-der - seht, wie - der-seht hier die - sen
65
CHORUS
Come a - way, fel-low sail - ors, come a -
Kommt an Bord, ihr Ma - tro - sen, kommt an
more. Come a - way, fel - low sail-ors, come a - way,
Strand. Kommt an Bord, ihr Ma - trosen, kommt an Bord,
come a - way, come a -
kommt an Bord, kommt an
Come a - way, fel - low sail - ors,
Kommt an Bord, ihr Ma - tro - sen,
Come a - way, fel - low sail - ors, come a - way,
Kommt an Bord, ihr Ma - tro - sen, kommt an Bord,
70
- way, your an - chors be weigh - ing, Time and tide will ad - mit no de -
Bord, die An - ker wir hie - ven, Zeit und Flut lässt uns län - ger nicht

75
- lay - ing. Take a booz - y short___ leave of your nymphs on the shore, And
blie - wen; Sagt ver - dammt kurz Leb - wohl Eu - ren Nym - phen am Land, Um -
80
si - lence their mourn - ing With vows of re - turn - ing, But nev - er in -
- fasst ih - re Mie - der, Ver - sprecht ihr kommt wie - der, Auch wenn ihr nie
85
- tend - ing to vis - it them more, no, nev - er in - tend - ing to vis - it them
wie - der - seht hier___ die - sen Strand, auch wenn ihr nie wie - der - seht hier die - sen

91
more, no, never, no, never intending to visit them more.
Strand, auch wenn ihr nie wiederseht, wiederseht hier diesen Strand.
The Sailors Dance
Matrosentanz
35
6
11
15
1.
2.

(Enter Sorceress and Witches)
(Zauberin und Hexen)
36
SORCERESS
See, see the flags and streamers curl - ing, Anchors weighing, sails un -
Sieh, sieh die Flag-gen, Wimpel weh - en, An - ker hoch, die Se - gel
4
FIRST WITCH
- furl-ing. Phoebe's pale de-lud - ing beams, Gild - ing o'er de - ceit - ful streams.
steh-en. Phoebes blas-ser Mor - gen-strahl, Gol - den färbt die Was - ser fahl.
SECOND WITCH
Our plot has took,
Der Plan ge - lang,
7
FIRST WITCH
E-lis - sa's ru-in'd, ho ho ho ho ho ho ho ho ho
E-lis - sas Ende, ho ho ho ho ho ho ho ho ho
The Queen's forsook, ho ho ho ho ho ho ho ho ho ho ho
Di-do ver-sank, ho ho ho ho ho ho ho ho ho ho ho

10
ho. E-lis - sa's ruin'd, ho—ho ho—ho ho– ho ho– ho ho– ho– ho–
ho. E-lis - sas Ende, ho—ho ho—ho ho– ho ho– ho ho– ho ho–
ho. E-lis - sa's ruin'd, ho—ho ho— ho ho– ho ho– ho– ho–
ho. E-lis - sas Ende, ho—ho ho— ho ho– ho ho– ho– ho–
13
ho. Our plot has took, our plot has took, The Queen's forsook, ho— ho ho—ho ho—
ho. Der Plan ge-lang, der Plan ge - lang, Di-do versank, ho— ho ho—ho ho—
ho. Our plot has took, The Queen's forsook, ho ho ho— ho ho—ho ho—
ho. Der Plan ge - lang, Di-do versank, ho ho ho— ho ho—ho ho—
16
ho. E-lis - sa's ruin'd, ho– ho ho— ho ho–ho–ho–ho ho ho ho ho.
ho. E-lis - sas Ende, ho– ho ho— ho ho–ho–ho–ho ho ho ho ho.
ho. E-lis - sa's ruin'd, ho– ho ho— ho ho– ho ho–ho–ho–ho–ho ho–ho– ho.
ho. E-lis - sas Ende, ho– ho ho— ho ho– ho ho–ho–ho–ho–ho ho–ho– ho.

37
SORCERESS
Our next mo - tion, Must be to storm
Un - ser Stre - ben, Muss sein im Sturm
her lov - er on the o - cean.
Ae - ne - as Un - heil zu we - ben.
1.
2.
o - cean. From the
we - ben. Aus dem
ru - in of o - thers our plea - sures we bor - row, E -
Un - glück der an - dern Ver - gnü - gen wir bor - gen, E -
lis - sa bleeds to - night, E - lis - sa bleeds
lis - sa stirbt heut' Nacht, E - lis - sa stirbt

16
to - night, And Car - thage flames to - mor-row. De -
heut' Nacht. Kar - tha - go flammt schon mor-gen. Ver -
struc-tion's our de - light, De - light our great-est sor-row, E - lis - sa dies to -
nicht-ungs-freud' uns lacht, Die Lust er-füllt mit Sor-gen, E - lis - sa stirbt heut'
6
- night, And Carthage flames to - morrow. Ho ho ho ho ho ho ho ho
Nacht, Kar - tha-go flammt schon morgen.
Ho ho ho ho ho
ho ho ho ho ho
Ho ho ho ho ho ho

11
ho— ho— ho.
ho. E - lis - sa dies to - night, And Car-thage flames to - mor - row. De -
ho— ho— ho. E - lis - sa stirbt heut' Nacht, Kar - tha - go flammt schon mor-gen. Ver -
ho— ho.
16
- struc-tion's our— de - light, De - light our great-est sor - row, E - lis - sa dies— to -
- nicht-ungs- freud' uns lacht, Die Lust er - füllt mit Sor - gen, E - lis - sa stirbt_heut'
Ho— ho—ho—ho ho—
21
- night, And—Carthage flames to - morrow. Ho— ho—ho—ho ho— ho ho—
Nacht, Kar - tha-go flammt schon morgen. Ho— ho— ho—ho ho—
Ho— ho—ho—ho ho— ho

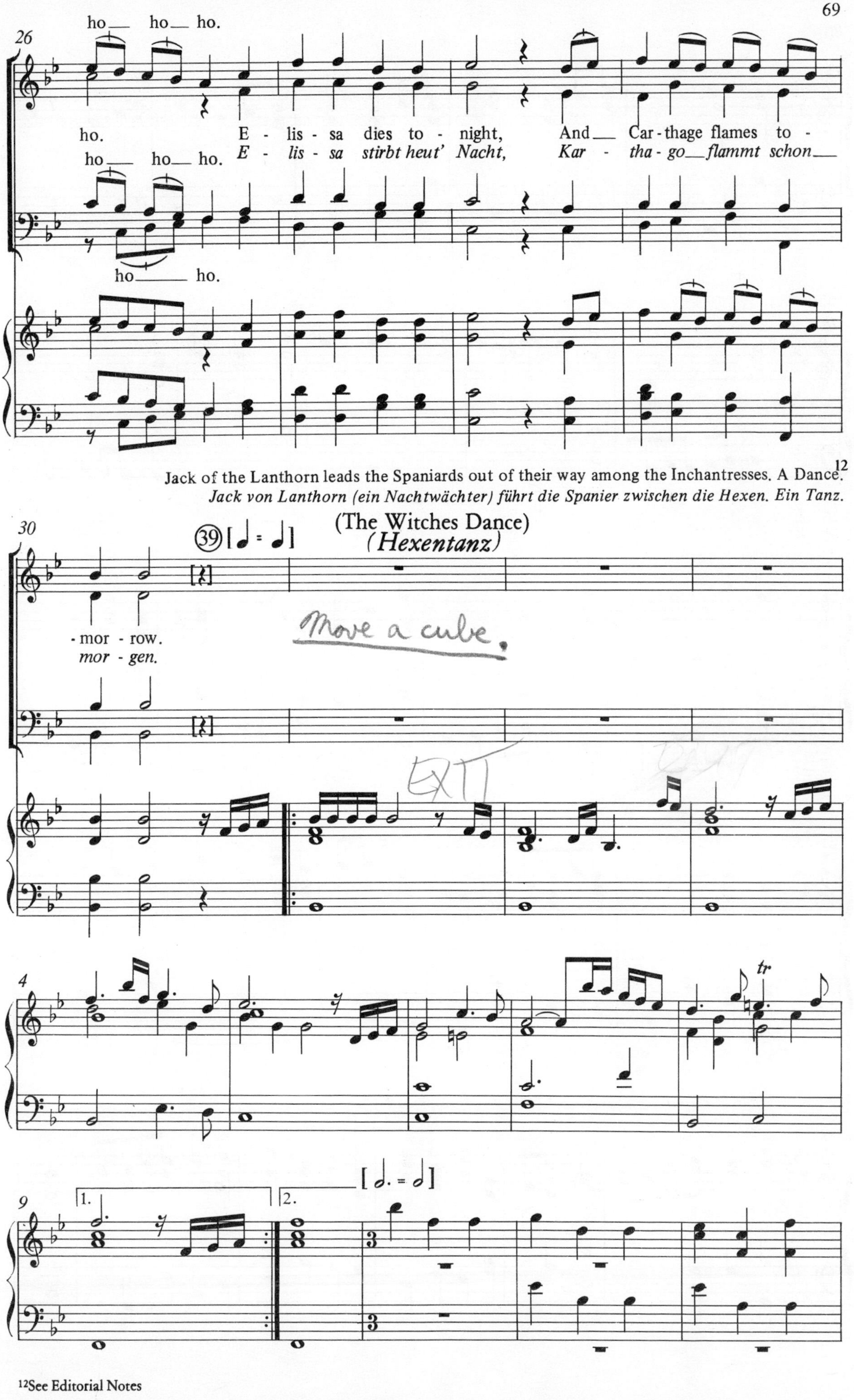

Jack of the Lanthorn leads the Spaniards out of their way among the Inchantresses. A Dance.[12]

Jack von Lanthorn (ein Nachtwächter) führt die Spanier zwischen die Hexen. Ein Tanz.

30

39 [♩ = ♩]

(The Witches Dance)

(Hexentanz)

- mor - row.

mor - gen.

Move a cube.

EXIT

4

9

1.

2.

[𝅗𝅥. = 𝅗𝅥]

[12]See Editorial Notes

Enter Dido, Belinda, and train. *Dido, Belinda, und Gefolgen.*

13 BELINDA Aeneas enters

re-fuge for the wretch - ed — left. See, Madam, see where the Prince ap-pears, Such
Zuflucht, die mir noch ge - hört. Sieh, Di-do, dort Ae-ne-as—kommt, Die

16

sor-row in his looks he bears, As would con - vince you still he's— true.
Trau-er sein-es Blik-kes frommt Dir zur Er - kennt-nis: Er ist— wahr.

18 AENEAS

What shall lost Ae - ne - as do. How, how,— roy - al
Nun bin ich des Glück - es bar. Wie, wie,— Schönste

21

fair, shall I impart The god's de-cree, and tell you we must part.
Du, soll ich nach Zeus' Gebot Dir sa - gen, dass ich jetzt scheiden muss?

24
DIDO
Thus on the fa - tal banks of Nile, Weeps the de - ceit - ful
So, nach dem al - ten Sa - gen - wort, Weint trü - ger - isch manch'
26
cro - co - dile. Thus hy - po-crites that mur - der act, Make heaven and gods the
Un - ge - heuer; Ich, Heuchler, ken - ne den Ver - rat, Nun gib den Göt - tern
28
AENEAS
DIDO
au - thors of the fact. By all that's good, By all that's good, no more. All that's
al - le Schuld der Tat. Beim höch-sten Gott, Beim höchsten Gott, ge-nug! Der höchste
31
good you have for - swore. To your promis'd Em-pire fly, And let for -
Gott kennt dei - nen Trug. Erreichst dein Ziel Du oh - ne Not, Wirst Du ver -

34 AENEAS

- sa - ken Di - do die. In spite of Jove's command — I'll stay, Offend the gods, and Love o -

- ges - sen Di - dos Tod. Ich tro-tze Zeus' Befehl, — ich bleib' Und ganz mich Deiner Lieb ver-

37 DIDO

- bey. No, faith-less man thy course pursue, I'm now re - solv'd — as well as you. No re -

- schreib'. Nein, Du be - trügst. Du musst nun gehn; Doch was ich will, — das bleibt bestehn. Kei - ne

40

- pen - tance shall re - claim, The in - jur'd Di - do's slight - ed flame. For 'tis e -

Reu - e ruf' zu - rück, Ge - kränk - ten Her - zens Lieb - es - glück. Es ist ge -

42

- nough, what-e'er — you — now de - cree, That you had once a

- nug, was Du — auch — jetzt be - schliesst, Dass Du ein - mal ge -

44
DIDO
thought of leav - ing me.
- dacht, dass Du mich fliehst.
AENEAS
Let Jove say what he will, I'll stay.
Trotz Zeus' Be - fehl: ich bleib' bei Dir.
A -
Fort,
47
- way, a - way! A - way, away! No, no, no, no, no,
fort von mir! Fort, fort von mir, Nein, nein, nein, nein, nein,
No, no, I'll stay. No, no, I'll stay. I'll stay, I'll stay,
Ich bleib' bei Dir, ich bleib' bei Dir, ich bleib' bei Dir,
50
no, a - way, a - way, a - way, a - way, a - way. To death I'll
nein, fort, fort von mir, fort, fort, von mir, fort, fort, Der Tod um -
I'll stay, and Love o - bey, I'll stay, and Love o - bey. I'll stay, I'll stay,
ich bleib', mein Lieb', bei Dir, ich bleib', mein Lieb', bei Dir, ich bleib', ich bleib',

53
fly if long-er you de-lay, a-way, a-way! But
-fängt mich hier wenn län-ger Du noch säumst, fort, fort von mir! Ich
Exit Aeneas
and Love o-bey, and Love o-bey.
mein Lieb, bei Dir, mein Lieb, bei Dir.
56
death, a-las, I can-not shun, Death must come when he is gone.
kann den Tod nicht mei-den: Er komm zu mir nach sei-nem Schei-den.
41
CHORUS
Great minds a-gainst them-selves con-spire, great minds, great
Hoch-sinn sich selbst oft wi-der-steht, Hoch-sinn, Hoch-
Great minds a-gainst them-selves con-spire, great minds, great
Hoch-sinn sich selbst oft wi-der-steht, Hoch-sinn, Hoch-
Great minds a-gainst them-selves con-spire, great minds, great
Hoch-sinn sich selbst oft wi-der-steht, Hoch-sinn, Hoch-
Great minds a-gainst them-selves con-spire, great minds,
Hoch-sinn sich selbst oft wi-der-steht, Hoch-sinn,
Violins

5
minds a-gainst, a-gainst them-selves con-spire, And shun the cure they most, they
-sinn sich selbst, sich selbst oft wi-der-steht, Und sieht den Weg nicht, der zum
minds a-gainst, a-gainst them-selves con-spire, And shun the
-sinn sich selbst, sich selbst oft wi-der-steht, Und sieht den
minds a-gainst, a-gainst them-selves con-spire, And shun the cure they
-sinn sich selbst, sich selbst oft wi-der-steht, Und sieht den Weg nicht,
great minds a-gainst them-selves con-spire,
Hoch-sinn sich selbst oft wi-der-steht,
9
most de-sire, and shun the cure they most de-sire, they most de-sire.
Hei-le geht, und sieht den Weg nicht, der zum Heile, der zum Hei-le geht.
cure, the cure, and shun the cure they most de-sire, the cure they most de-sire.
Weg nicht, der zum Hei-le geht, und sieht den Weg nicht, der zum Hei-le geht.
most de-sire, and shun the cure they most, they most de-sire.
Hei-le geht, und sieht den Weg nicht, der zum Hei-le geht.
And shun the cure they most de-sire, and shun the cure they most de-sire.
Und sieht den Weg des Hei-les nicht, den Weg nicht, der zum Hei-le geht.

42
DIDO
Thy hand, Be - lin - da, dark - - - ness shades me, On thy
Führ mich, Be - lin - da! durch dunk - - - le Schat - ten, Lass mich
4
bos - om let me rest, More I would but death in -
ru - hen, läch - elnd fast, Fühl' ich schon ein süss' Er -
7
43
- vades me. Death is now a wel - come guest.
- mat - ten? Tod, sei mir will-komm' - ner Gast.
2
When I am
Werd' ich ins
Violins very Soft

7
laid, am laid in earth, may my wrongs cre - ate no
Grab, ins Grab ge - legt, schaff mein Lei - - den nicht viel
12
trou - ble, no trou - ble in thy breast. When I am
Kum - mer, viel Kum - mer Dei - nem Sinn. Werd' ich ins
17
laid, am laid in earth, may my wrongs cre - ate no
Grab, ins Grab ge - legt, schaff mein Lei - - den nicht viel
22
trou - ble, no trou - ble in thy breast. Re - mem-ber me,
Kum -- mer, viel Kum - mer Dei - nem Sinn. Ge - den -ke mein,

27
re - mem-ber me, but ah! forget my
ge - den - ke mein, doch, ah! vergiss mein
32
fate, re - member me, but ah! for - get my fate. Re -
Los, ge - den-ke mein, doch, ah! ver - giss mein Los. Ge -
37
- mem - ber me, re - member me, but ah! for-get my
- den - ke mein, ge - den-ke mein, doch ah! vergiss mein
42
fate, re - member me, but ah! for - get my fate.
Los, ge - den-ke mein, doch ah! ver - giss mein Los.
Rit-

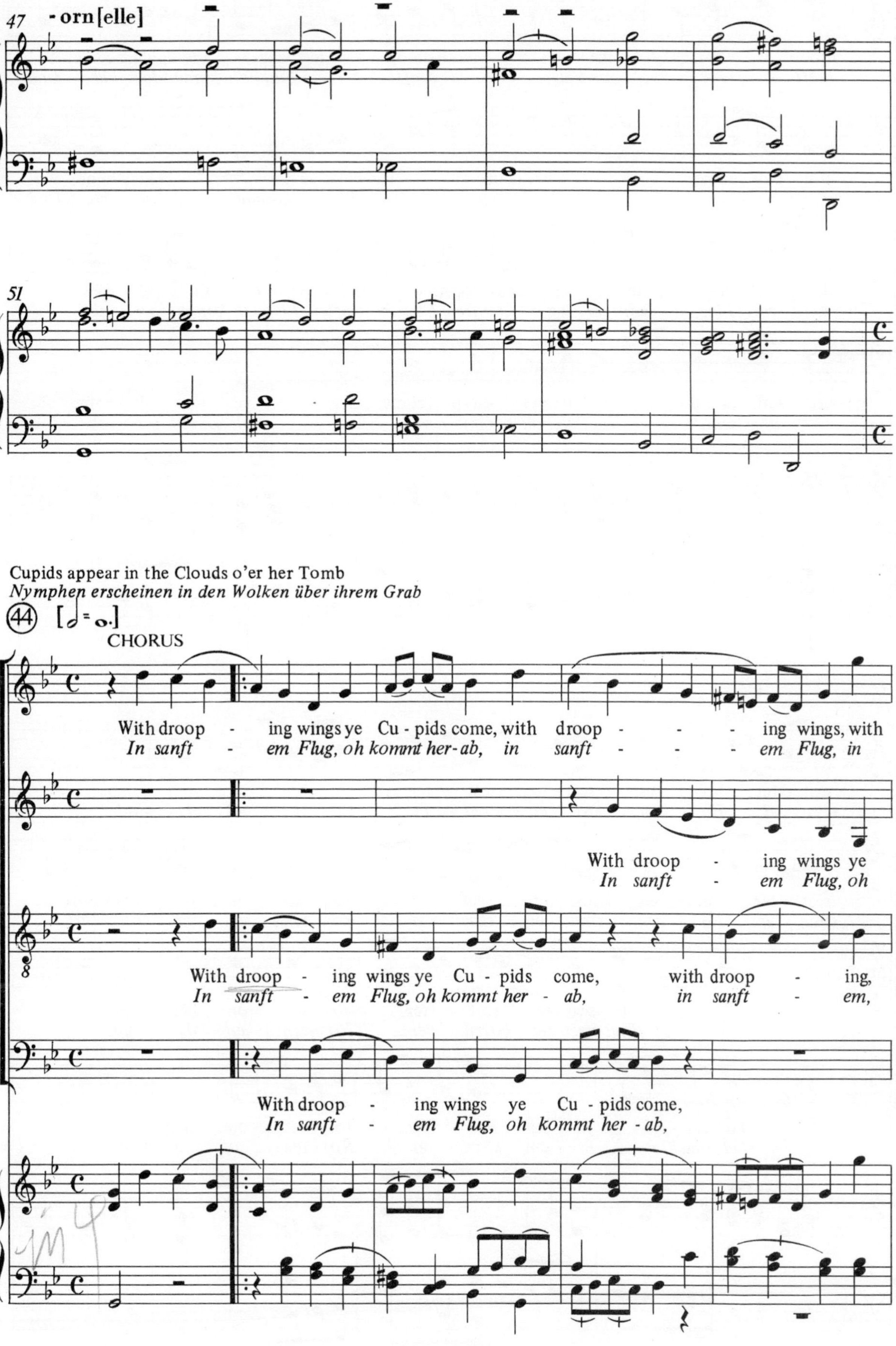

Cupids appear in the Clouds o'er her Tomb

Nymphen erscheinen in den Wolken über ihrem Grab

(44) [𝅗𝅥 = 𝅝.]

CHORUS

With droop - ing wings ye Cu - pids come, with droop - - - ing wings, with

In sanft - em Flug, oh kommt her-ab, in sanft - - - em Flug, in

With droop - ing wings ye

In sanft - em Flug, oh

With droop - ing wings ye Cu - pids come, with droop - ing,

In sanft - em Flug, oh kommt her - ab, in sanft - em,

With droop - ing wings ye Cu - pids come,

In sanft - em Flug, oh kommt her - ab,

droop - - - ing wings, with droop - ing wings ye Cu - pids_ come, To
sanft - - - em Flug, in sanft - em Flug, oh kommt her - ab, Und
Cu - pids come, with droop - ing wings ye Cu - - pids come, To
kommt her - ab, in sanft - em Flug,oh kommt_ her - ab, Und
droop-ing wings, with drooping wings, with drooping wings, with drooping wings ye Cu - pids come,
sanft - em Flug, in sanftem Flug, in sanftem Flug, in sanftem Flug, oh kommt her - ab,
with droop - ing wings ye Cu-pids come,_ ye Cu - pids come,
In sanft - em Flug, oh kommt her-ab,_ oh kommt her - ab,
scat - ter_ ro - ses, scat - ter,_scat - ter_ ro - ses_ on_ her tomb.
streu - et_ Ro - sen, streu - et,_streu - et_ Ro - sen_ auf_ ihr Grab.
scat - ter_ ro - ses, scat - ter,_ scat - ter_ ro - ses on her tomb. Soft,_
streu - et_ Ro - sen, streu - et,_ streu - et_ Ro - sen auf ihr Grab. Zart_
To scat - ter,_scat - ter_ ro - ses on her tomb.
Und streu - et,_streu - et_ Ro - sen auf ihr Grab.
To scat - ter_ ro - ses, scat - ter_ ro - ses_ on her tomb.
Und streu - et_ Ro - sen, streu - et_ Ro - sen_ auf ihr Grab.

15
Soft, soft and gen - tle, soft,
Zart, zart ihr Her - ze zart,
soft and gen - tle as her heart, gen - tle as her heart,
zart und fein ihr Her - ze war, zart ihr Her - ze war,
Soft, soft, soft and gen - tle as her heart,
Zart, zart, zart und fein ihr Her - ze war,
Soft, soft and gen - tle, soft, soft,
Zart und fein ihr Her - ze war, zart,
19
soft, soft, soft and gen - tle as her heart, Keep here,
zart, zart, zart und fein ihr Her - ze war, Und hier
soft, soft, soft and gen - tle, gen - tle as her heart, Keep here,
zart, zart, zart und fein ihr Her - - - ze war, Und hier
soft, soft and gen - tle as her heart, Keep here,
zart, zart und fein ihr Her - ze war, Und hier
soft, soft, soft and gen - tle as her heart, Keep here,
zart, zart, zart und fein ihr Her - ze war, Und hier

here your watch, keep here, here, keep here your watch, and ne-ver, ne-ver,
hal - tet Wacht, und hier, hier, hier hal - tet Wacht, auf immer, im-mer,
Cupids' Dance[13]
Amorettentanz
[2nd time instruments only]
1.
2.
ne - ver part, and ne-ver, ne-ver, ne - ver, ne - ver part.
im - mer-dar, auf immer, im-mer, im - mer, immer - dar.

FINIS

APPENDIX

⑬ A Dance Gittars Chacony

Gitarrentanz (Chaconne)

31
37
[tr]
43
(28) Gitter ground a Dance
Gitarrentanz (Chaconne)
tr
tr
7
13